Thinking Through The Test

A Study Guide

to accompany

THE FLORIDA COLLEGE BASIC SKILLS EXIT TESTS: READING

D. J. Henry
Daytona Beach Community College

Mimi Markus
Broward Community College

Longman

New York Boston San Francisco
London Toronto Sydney Tokyo Singapore Madrid
Mexico City Munich Paris Cape Town Hong Kong Montreal

Thinking Through the Test: A Study Guide to accompany *The Florida College Basic Skills Exit Tests: Reading*

ISBN: 0-321-27746-5

2 3 4 5 6 7 8 9 10–ML–07 06 05 04

CONTENTS

PREFACE

To the Student

For many of you, test taking is a most stressful and fearful task. Weeks and months of hard work and significant learning can seem to fly away in a single test session. The purpose of *Thinking Through the Test* is to help lessen your anxiety and strengthen your skills as you prepare for and take the Florida College Basic Skills Exit Tests for Reading.

First of all, you should take comfort in the fact that community college teachers who are actively teaching reading and writing in classrooms throughout the state write the state exit exam. So the skills addressed on the test and in this workbook are the skills that you are studying in your classrooms, textbooks, and learning centers. In fact, the purpose of this book is *not* to teach the test, but to support the instruction and learning that you need to be a successful college student.

In order to support your classroom instruction and prepare you for the college classroom, passages for the items in this workbook have been taken from textbooks currently used in freshman college classes. The passages also represent a variety of content courses, such as biological sciences, social sciences, history, study skills, government, and education. Because these passages are taken from college-level textbooks that you could be reading in the near future, they may contain unfamiliar concepts and words and, in all likelihood, will be more difficult than the passages on the actual state tests. So be sure to use the workbook as an opportunity to apply the new skills you are acquiring from your reading and writing classes. Study smart; always make connections between skills and learning tasks.

One of the benefits of this workbook is that the exercises are very similar to the items you will face on the state tests. Therefore, some of the same passages appear in several chapters, for the state exam uses a single passage to ask several types of questions. For example, there are ten passages in chapter one of the Reading Workbook on main ideas; those same passages or portions of them are also in other chapters: the same passage, different questions. This repetition should help you see the connections between skills, questions, and the benefit of re-reading for better understanding.

Study smart and make connections whenever possible. Answer sheets have been included to help you track your progress and record your own thinking about your reasons for the choices you make in each activity. The more you *think through* your learning, the more likely you are to be successful on the state test and in your future college courses.

Part One: Diagnostic Reading Test

Read the passage below and answer the questions that follow.

Carnivorous plants trap their prey, which may vary from single-celled organisms, small crustaceans, mosquito larvae, and tiny water insects to small tadpoles, large insects, and small amphibians. Carnivorous plants fall into two groups. Active trappers use rapid plant movements to open trap doors or to close traps. Passive trappers use pitfalls or sticky

5   adhesive traps.

Two examples of active trappers are the Venus flytrap and the aquatic and semi-aquatic bladderworts. The Venus flytrap uses clam-shaped, hinged leaves. Around their unattached edges are many guard hairs and very small nectar glands that attract insects. On the surface of each half are three small trigger hairs and a covering of small digestive

10   glands. An insect attracted to the brightly colored leaf touches the trigger hairs, causing the trap to close quickly. The bladderwort, as its name suggests, has small, elastic, flattened bladders with the entrance sealed by a flap of cells. When prey touch the tactile cells on the flap, the trap door opens. The bladder walls spring apart, causing a sucking motion that sweeps a current of water into the bladder. Then the door closes, trapping the

15   prey.

Pitcher plants and sundews are examples of passive trappers. Pitcher plants use pitfalls. The leaves are shaped into pitcher-like or funnel-like traps that grow from underground stems. Bright coloration and secretions of nectar attract the insects. When they land and move down the leaf, the insects are unable to back up against the stiff, downward-

20   directed hairs. They fall into watery fluid containing digestive enzymes produced by the leaf. The sundews attract insects to sticky leaves by color, scent, and glistening droplets of adhesive. Sundews have two types of glands on the leaf surface that produce adhesive droplets. Long stalks on the edge of the leaf trap the insect. Shorter stalks slowly bend into the center of the leaf, holding the prey in the digestive area of the leaf. (Adapted from Smith, Robert Leo, and Thomas M. Smith. *Elements of Ecology*. 5th ed. San Francisco: Benjamin Cummings, 2003)

1.   Which sentence best states the main idea of the passage?
      A.   Carnivorous plans eat a variety of insects, tadpoles, small amphibians, and small crustaceans.
      B.   The bright colors of carnivorous plants attract insects and other small creatures.
      C.   Carnivorous plants contain digestive enzymes in their leaves that help them take in nutrients from their prey.
      D.   Carnivorous plants use a trapping process to catch their prey.

2.   The author's purpose is to
      A.   explain how the different types of carnivorous plants trap their prey.
      B.   define carnivorous plants.
      C.   contrast active trappers with passive trappers.
      D.   explain the effects of being caught in a carnivorous plant.

1

3. "Carnivorous plants trap their prey, which may vary from single celled organisms, small crustaceans, mosquito larvae, and tiny water insects to small tadpoles, large insects, and small amphibians." (lines 1-3)

   The relationship of parts within the sentence above is
   A. contrast.
   B. addition.
   C. example.
   D. summary.

4. "When they land and move down the leaf, the insects are unable to back up against the stiff, downward-directed hairs. They fall into watery fluid containing digestive enzymes produced by the leaf." (lines 18-21)

   Identify the relationship between these two sentences from paragraph three.
   A. process
   B. time
   C. comparison
   D. cause/effect

5. In this passage, the author shows bias in favor of
   A. the variety of different carnivorous plants.
   B. the ability of carnivorous plants to catch prey.
   C. the beauty of carnivorous plants.
   D. the gruesome process carnivorous plants use to catch prey.

6. What is the overall tone of this passage?
   A. excited
   B. authoritative
   C. informational
   D. convincing

7. "The bladderwort, as its name suggests, has small, elastic, flattened bladders with the entrance sealed by a flap of cells." (lines 11-12)

   The above sentence is a statement of
   A. fact.
   B. opinion.

8. A conclusion that can be drawn from the third paragraph is that sundews
   A. have different types of leaves.
   B. use color, scent, and sticky droplets to attract prey.
   C. use their two types of stalks to hold the prey.
   D. are similar to Venus flytraps.

9. Throughout the passage, which type of support is offered for to describe the types of carnivorous plants?
   A. objective
   B. emotional

Read the passage below and answer the questions that follow.

Karen Silkwood grew up in an unassuming middle-class family in Nederland, Texas, near the Gulf Coast. She baby-sat at her church nursery, earned straight A's through high school, and went to Lamar College on a full scholarship to study medical technology. Marriage, three children, and a divorce intervened, and in 1972, she began working as a
5   laboratory analyst at Kerr-McGee's plutonium processing plant in Crescent, Oklahoma. There the highly poisonous radioactive material was made into fuel rods for nuclear power plants.

In the summer of 1974, at age 28, Silkwood was elected a local official of the union that represented many Kerr-McGee workers and began organizing for greater worker safety.
10   She learned of numerous incidents of radioactive contamination at the plant. She also uncovered evidence of significant quantities of missing plutonium. On November 13, Silkwood set out for Oklahoma City to meet a national representative of her union and a *New York Times* reporter, intending to give them documents proving that Kerr-McGee was knowingly manufacturing defective nuclear products. She never made it. Her car
15   was forced off the road, and she died instantly when it crashed into a concrete culvert.

Karen Silkwood challenged the power of one of the nation's largest energy corporations and paid with her life. Her brief career as a whistleblower brought together major issues of the 1970s: labor organizing, environmental damage, the safety record of nuclear energy, and the power of corporations over individual citizens. Her dismissive treatment
20   by some fellow workers, her employers, and the media also suggested the lack of respect that women had long endured, especially when they moved out of the role of the traditional homemaker. (Jones, Jacqueline, et al. *Created Equal*. New York: Longman, 2003)

10. Which statement best matches the main idea of the passage?
    A.   Karen Silkwood was concerned about workers' safety at the Kerr-McGee plant.
    B.   Karen Silkwood's treatment by workers and employees showed discrimination against working women.
    C.   Karen Silkwood was killed for exposing radioactive contamination at the Kerr-McGee plant.
    D.   As a whistleblower, Karen Silkwood brought to light the major issues of the 1970s.

11. Karen Silkwood's reason for working as a local official of the union was
    A.   to get her name in the *New York Times*.
    B.   to expose incidents of radioactive contamination in the plant.
    C.   to get a promotion in the company.
    D.   to get experience as a labor organizer.

12. The primary purpose of this passage is to
    A. tell the story of how Silkwood tried to expose her employer's underhanded practices.
    B. give the effects of working in a plutonium processing plant.
    C. argue against whistleblowing.
    D. evaluate the importance of exposing hazardous working conditions.

13. For this passage, the author uses an overall organizational pattern of
    A. example.
    B. contrast.
    C. narration.
    D. spatial order.

14. "She baby-sat at her church nursery, earned straight A's through high school, and went to Lamar College on a full scholarship to study medical technology." (lines 2-3)

    The relationship of the parts within the sentence above is
    A. cause and effect.
    B. example.
    C. praise.
    D. simple listing.

15. As used in line 19, the word <u>dismissive</u> most nearly means
    A. accepting.
    B. indifferent.
    C. hateful.
    D. violent

16. The tone of this passage can be described as
    A. admiring.
    B. optimistic.
    C. neutral.
    D. sad.

17. "Her dismissive treatment by some fellow workers, her employers, and the media also suggested the lack of respect that women had long endured, especially when they moved out of the role of the traditional homemaker." (lines 19-22)

    The above sentence is a statement of
    A. fact.
    B. opinion.

18. A conclusion that can be drawn from the passage is that
    A. whistleblowers risk their jobs and their lives.
    B. in the 1970s, women were expected to be traditional homemakers.
    C. Silkwood tried to expose Kerr-McGee's dangerous practices but died in the process.
    D. working in a plutonium processing plant is hazardous.

4

Read the passage below and answer the questions that follow.

Research in Japan on the personality of the "salarymen" males employed in the fast-paced corporate world, links male personality with the demands of the business world. Salarymen work long hours for the company. They leave home early in the morning and return late at night and thus are nicknamed "7-11 men."

5   Many Tokyo salarymen eat dinner with their family only a few times a year. After work, they typically spend many hours with fellow workers at expensive nightclubs. Groups of about five to ten men go out together after work. A few drinks and light snacks can result in a tab in the hundreds of dollars for one hour. The corporation picks up the bill. At the club, men relax and have fun after a long day of work. This is ensured by having a trained
10   hostess sit at the table, keeping the conversation moving along in a lightly playful tone. Her job is to flatter and flirt with the men and to make them feel good.

    While working as a hostess, one woman found that conversations are full of teasing and banter, with much of it directed at the hostess. This may be viewed as a reaction to their upbringing, with its total control by the mother. Club culture puts the man in control. The
15   hostess can flirt with him but she will never control him.

    Salarymen's night club behavior appears to be linked with their upbringing. Given the near total absence of the father from the home scene, children are raised mainly by the mother. The concentration of maternal attention is especially strong toward sons and their school achievements. The goal is that the boy will do well in school, get into a top
20   university, and then gain employment with a large corporation. These corporations pay well, guarantee lifelong employment, and provide substantial benefits after retirement. Loyalty is required, work hours are long, and the pressure to perform is high. (Adapted from Miller, Barbara D. *Cultural Anthropology*. 2nd ed. Boston: Allyn and Bacon, 2002)

19.   Which sentence best states the main idea of this passage?
    A.   Salarymen spend little time at home with their families.
    B.   Japanese corporations pay well and offer security and excellent retirement benefits.
    C.   Salarymen's night club behavior appears to be linked with their upbringing.
    D.   Children of salarymen are raised primarily by their mothers.

20.   The implied main idea of paragraph two is
    A.   corporations reward salarymen for working hard all day by paying for their evening entertainment in clubs.
    B.   salarymen prefer socializing with their fellow workers after work than going home to their families.
    C.   corporations support family values.
    D.   salarymen do not care about their families.

21. According to the passage, the hostess
    A.   is in total control of the men.
    B.   encourages the men to buy drinks.
    C.   has to accept insulting remarks from the men to keep them happy.
    D.   is trained to keep the conversation going.

22. For this passage, the author uses the overall organizational pattern that
    A.   compares husbands' and wives' roles in Japan.
    B.   suggests reasons for salarymen's nightclub behavior.
    C.   describes what salarymen do.
    D.   gives examples of what salarymen do at clubs.

23. What is the relationship between the parts of the following sentence?

    "Given the near total absence of the father from the home scene, children are raised mainly by the mother." (lines 16-18)
    A.   cause and effect
    B.   contrast
    C.   process
    D.   time order

24. Identify the relationship between these two sentences in paragraph three:

    "While working as a hostess, one woman found that conversations are full of teasing and banter, with much of it directed at the hostess. This may be viewed as a reaction to their upbringing, with its total control by the mother." (lines 12-14)
    A.   contrast
    B.   time order
    C.   cause and effect
    D.   clarification

25. The word banter (line 13) means
    A.   flatter.
    B.   poke fun at.
    C.   soothe.
    D.   bully.

26. What is the overall tone of this passage?
    A.   complaining
    B.   humorous
    C.   lofty
    D.   subjective

27. The author's claim that "after work, they typically spend many hours with fellow workers at expensive nightclubs" (lines 5-6) is
    A.   inadequately supported because it depends on personal opinion.
    B.   adequately supported by factual evidence.

Read the passage below and answer the questions that follow.

Silence communicates. Silence allows the speaker time to think, time to formulate and organize his or her verbal communications. Silence also seems to prepare the receiver for the importance of these future messages.

5   Some people use silence as a weapon to hurt others. We often speak of giving someone "the silent treatment." After a conflict, for example, one or both individuals might remain silent as a kind of punishment. Silence used to hurt others may also take the form of refusing to acknowledge the presence of another person; in this case silence is a dramatic demonstration of the total indifference one person feels towards another.

10   Sometimes silence is used as a response to personal anxiety, shyness, or threats. You may feel anxious or shy among new people and prefer to remain silent. By remaining silent, you preclude the chance of rejection.

Silence may be used to prevent communication of certain messages. In conflict situations, silence is sometimes used to prevent certain topics from surfacing to prevent one or both parties from saying things they may later regret. In such situations, silence often allows
15   us time to cool off before expressing hatred, severe criticism, or personal attacks, which, we know, are irreversible.

Another way silence can be used is to communicate emotional responses. It may communicate determination to be uncooperative or defiant. Your silence defies the authority of the other person. Silence also communicates annoyance. Silence may express
20   affection or love, especially when coupled with long stares into each other's eyes.

Of course, you may also use silence when you simply have nothing to say, when nothing occurs to you, or when you do not want to say anything. (Adapted from DeVito, Joseph. *Essentials of Human Communication*. New York: Longman, 1999)

28.   Which sentence best states the main idea of this passage?
       A.   Silence gives a speaker time to think.
       B.   Silence can be used to communicate many different messages.
       C.   Using silence as a punishment is hurtful.
       D.   Silence has dramatic effects.

29.   According to the passage, silence
       A.   can prevent people from saying things they may regret.
       B.   is a helpful tool.
       C.   is necessary in communication situations.
       D.   should be encouraged.

30.   For this passage, the author uses the organizational pattern that
       A.   contrasts using silence to hurt with using silence to help.
       B.   gives a definition of silence.
       C.   argues for the use of silence.
       D.   classifies types of silence according to their purpose.

31. The second paragraph is organized by
   A. analyzing the effects of hurtful silence.
   B. examining similarities in hurtful silence behaviors.
   C. giving examples of using silence to hurt someone.
   D. arguing that the silent treatment is hurtful.

32. What is the relationship between the parts of the following sentence?

   "Silence used to hurt others may also take the form of refusing to acknowledge the presence of another person; in this case silence is a dramatic demonstration of the total indifference one person feels towards another." (lines 6-8)
   A. clarification
   B. comparison
   C. summary
   D. example

33. As used in line 18, the word <u>defiant</u> nearly means
   A. mean.
   B. resistant.
   C. cool.
   D. egotistical.

34. The author shows bias in favor of
   A. thinking before speaking.
   B. silent resistance.
   C. the ways silence communicates.
   D. using silence to hurt someone.

35. "Silence also seems to prepare the receiver for the importance of these future messages." (lines 2-3)

   The above sentence is a statement of
   A. fact.
   B. opinion.

36. A conclusion that can be drawn from this passage is that
   A. silence helps people think.
   B. people use silence to protect themselves.
   C. silence has many benefits.
   D. silence is a communication tool that has positive and negative uses.

Part Two: Reading Workbook

CHAPTER 1: *CONCEPT SKILLS*

1
The Main Idea:
Thesis Statement and Topic Sentences

This section tests your ability to determine the implied or stated main idea of a passage or paragraph. You must be able to distinguish the main idea from details, misinterpretations, inferences, and partial statements of the main idea.

In test questions identifying main ideas, misinterpretations and improper inferences *often* provide tricky false choices because they imitate the main idea. Keep in mind differences between the function and characteristics of statements of main ideas, misinterpretations, and inferences. Remember that the **main idea** is the most important idea in the passages. The **thesis statement** or **topic sentence** controls the entire passage and serves as the basis upon which all other ideas are built. Every sentence, every detail, must be directly or indirectly related to the main idea.

EXAMPLE: Notice in the following passage the underlined topic sentence. The main idea focuses on transformation, or great change, in a specific place (Western society) over a specific time span (sixteenth through eighteenth centuries). Notice, too, the reinforcement of this controlling idea. The italicized words illustrate those sentences *directly* related to the topic sentence. The remaining sentences (the last three of the first paragraph) provide indirect support.

Great transformations had taken place in Western society between the beginning of the sixteenth century and the end of the eighteenth. The *Reformation* had shattered the *unity* of Christendom, and the *Enlightenment* had *challenged* the *roots* of Christian belief itself. The *European economy* had acquired a *global dimension* through the conquest and exploitation of the New World and the *expansion* of its markets in Asia and Africa. The *scientific revolution* had *reordered* Western people's *views* of the cosmos and themselves. Yet the political order of Europe had remained static. The nations of Europe were still governed by monarchs and princes. The nobility was still predominant; its privileges seemingly more entrenched than ever.

The French Revolution challenged all that. Within a matter of weeks in the summer of 1789, a social and political *edifice* that had stood for *1,000 years* was *torn down*, and for a generation all of Europe was caught up in the *convulsive changes* that ensued. From the very beginning, the revolution was recognized as the most important event of the age. In its *turmoil* and *agony* the *shape* of the modern world first *became visible*. (Greaves, Richard L., Robert Zaller, and Jennifer Tolbert Roberts. *Civilizations of the West: The Human Adventure: Volume C: From the French Revolution to the Present.* 597-598)

In contrast, a **misinterpretation** explains the data incorrectly and offers a misleading summary of the content of the passage's details.

EXAMPLE: *The French Revolution was the single most important event that led to tremendous transformations in Western society.*

The above statement is a good example of a misinterpretation of the data in the preceding example paragraph. The passage does clearly state that the French Revolution is the most important event to reshape Western civilization; however, the passage also clearly includes a number of other factors as well, such as the Reformation, the Enlightenment, and European global expansion. The inclusion of one word "single" makes the above statement a misrepresentation of the passage's main idea. Additionally, the original sentence in the passage is a statement of indirect (or secondary) support because it characterizes the French Revolution as an *example* of the *change* mentioned in the topic sentence.

- An improper **inference** is an assumption, or taking for granted as truth, a conclusion that may not be supported by the information.

EXAMPLE: *Greed and pride led to the great social upheavals within Western society between the beginning of the sixteenth century and the end of the eighteenth.*

The above statement is an improper inference based on the passage above. Though such words as "economy, expansion, and exploitation" may imply or suggest greed, there is not sufficient, specific information to form such a harsh opinion. Additionally, the concepts of "Reformation, Enlightenment" or even "revolution" require much more explanation to justify the assumption of pride as the challenge to traditional Christian or political authority.

Both misinterpretations and improper inferences can be broad statements that seem to address the points in the passage; however, they will either twist the author's meaning or go beyond what the author intended to imply.

You will be presented with a passage and then asked to choose which sentence best states its main idea, or you may be asked to choose the sentence that best expresses the implied main idea. Be sure to choose the option that all the details of the passage supports or explains.

- The main idea, thesis statement, or topic sentence may be in one of three locations: at the beginning, in the middle, or at the end of a passage. Look for the sentence that is broad enough to include all the major points and possibly the pattern of development. For example, sentences that include summaries of causes, results, types, comparisons, or contrasts are often main idea statements.

Exercises: Main Ideas

PASSAGE #1
Read the passage below and answer the following questions.

1   Although many people think of First Ladies as well-dressed homemakers presiding over White House dinners, there is much more to the job. The First Lady has no official government position. Yet she is often at the center of national attention. The media chronicles every word she speaks and every hairstyle she adopts.

5   Abigail Adams (an early feminist) and Dolly Madison counseled and lobbied their husbands. Edith Galt Wilson was the most powerful First lady, virtually running the government when her husband, Woodrow, suffered a paralyzing stroke in 1919. Eleanor Roosevelt wrote a nationally syndicated newspaper column and tirelessly traveled and advocated New Deal policies. She became her crippled husband's eyes and ears around
10   the country and urged him to adopt liberal social welfare policies. Lady Bird Johnson chose to focus on one issue, beautification, and most of her successors followed this pattern. Rosalyn Carter chose mental health, Nancy Reagan selected drugs, and Barbara Bush picked literacy.

    In what was perhaps a natural evolution in a society where women have moved into
15   positions formerly held only by males, Hillary Rodham Clinton attained the most responsible and visible leadership position ever held by a First Lady. She had been an influential advisor to the President, playing an active role in the selection of nominees for cabinet and judicial posts, for example. Most publicly, she headed the planning for the President's massive health care reform plan in 1993 and became, along with her husband,
20   its primary advocate. (Adapted from Edwards, George C., Martin P. Wattenberg, and Robert L. Lineberry. *Government in America.* 9th ed. New York: Longman, 2000)

1.   The implied idea of the entire passage is that
    A. The job of First Lady reflects the role of women in society at the time.
    B. The role of First Lady has become more important in the past 50 years.
    C. First Ladies have taken active roles during their husbands' presidencies.
    D. The media reports all of the First Ladies' activities.

2.   Which of the following sentences best states the main idea of paragraph 2?
    A. Some First Ladies focused on one issue while others were more involved in helping the President run the government.
    B. Edith Galt Wilson was the most powerful First Lady.
    C. Eleanor Roosevelt helped her husband run the government because he was disabled.
    D. First Ladies are champions of causes.

3.   The implied idea of paragraph 3 is that
    A. Hillary Rodham Clinton was a model First Lady.
    B. Hillary Rodham Clinton planned the health care reform plan in 1993.
    C. Hillary Rodham Clinton was well educated.
    D. Hillary Rodham Clinton held the most responsible leadership position of all First Ladies.

PASSAGE #2

Read the passage below and answer the following questions.

1   "Street gangs" are a more formal variety of youth gang. They generally have leaders and a hierarchy of membership roles and responsibilities. They are named, and their members mark their identity with tattoos or "colors." While many street gangs are involved in violence, not all are. An anthropologist who did research among nearly forty street gangs

5   in New York, Los Angeles, and Boston learned much about why individuals join gangs, providing insights that contradict popular thinking on this subject.

     One common stereotype is that young boys join gangs because they are from homes with no male authority figure with whom they could identify. This study showed that equal numbers of gang members were from intact nuclear households as from those with an

10   absent father. Another common perception is that the gang replaces a missing feeling of family as a motive. This study, again, showed that the same number of gang members reported having close family ties as those who did not.

     Those who were gang members shared a personality type called a "defiant individualist." This type has five traits: intense competitiveness, mistrust or wariness, self-reliance,

15   social isolation, and a strong survival instinct. Poverty, especially urban poverty, leads to the development of this type of personality. Many of these youths want to be economically successful, but social conditions channel their interests and skills into illegal pursuits rather than into legal pathways of achievement. (Adapted from Miller, Barbara D. *Cultural Anthropology*. 2nd ed. Boston: Allyn and Bacon, 2002)

4.   Which of the following sentences is the best statement of the main idea in the entire passage?
     A. The reasons individuals join street gangs are not those commonly held.
     B. An anthropologist studied street gangs in New York, Los Angeles, and Boston.
     C. Not all street gangs are involved in violence.
     D. Street gangs are a type of youth gang that is organized and identifies itself with "colors."

5.   The implied main idea of paragraph 3 is that
     A. Street gang members are victims of society.
     B. Street gang members would be successful if they weren't poor.
     C. Street gang members are not competitive.
     D. Individuals develop a "defiant individualist" personality type due to urban poverty.

6.   The implied meaning of paragraph 2 is that
     A. many gang members have close family ties.
     B. most gang members have no male authority figures in the household.
     C. individuals do not join gangs for the reasons most people think.
     D. people think that the gang is a substitute for a missing family, but this is not true.

PASSAGE #3
Read the passage below and then answer the questions that follow.

1   In the 1980s, a long-running TV public service advertisement showed a father confronting his son with what is obviously the boy's drug paraphernalia. The father asks his son incredulously, "Where did you learn to do this?" The son, half in tears, replies, "From you, okay? I learned it from watching you!" Observational learning, which results

5   simply from watching others, clearly appears to be a factor in an adolescent's willingness to experiment with drugs and alcohol.

Andrews and her colleagues found that adolescents' relationships with their parents influence whether they will model the substance use patterns of the parents. Specifically, they found that adolescents who had a positive relationship with their mothers modeled

10   her use (or nonuse) of cigarettes, and those who had a close relationship with their fathers modeled the father's marijuana use (or nonuse). Similarly, those who had a negative relationship with their parents were less likely to model their parents' use of drugs or alcohol. Although some of the more complex results of this study depended on the age and sex of the adolescent, the general findings can be understood by thinking about them

15   from the three levels of analysis and their interactions.

At the level of the brain, observing someone engage in a behavior causes you to store new memories, which involves the hippocampus and related brain systems. These memories later can guide behavior, as they do in all types of imitation. At the level of the person, if you are motivated to observe someone, you are likely to be paying more

20   attention to him or her and, therefore, increasing the likelihood of your learning from them and remembering what you learn. At the level of the group, you are more likely to be captivated by models who have certain attractive characteristics.

In this case, adolescents who had a positive relationship with their parents were more likely to do what their parents did; if their parents didn't smoke, the adolescents were less

25   likely to do so. The events at these levels interact. Children who enjoy a positive relationship with their parents may agree with their parents higher status than do children who have a negative relationship with their parents. Thus, the former group of children probably increases the amount of attention they give to their parents' behavior. (Adapted from Kosslyn, Stephen M., and Robin S. Rosenberg. *Psychology*. 2nd ed. Boston: Allyn and Bacon, 2004)

7.   Which of the following sentences is the best statement of the main idea of the entire passage?
     A. Your brain stores memories of observing someone's behavior.
     B. Children who have a positive relationship with their parents pay more attention to the way their parents act.
     C. A parent's use of drugs or alcohol will cause the child to use these substances.
     D. Watching people behaving a certain way on television becomes stored in your memory.

8. The implied idea of paragraph 4 is
   A. if a parent smokes, the adolescent will smoke.
   B. the parent-child relationship affects the child's behavior.
   C. children who have a negative relationship with their parents are likely to copy their parents' behavior.
   D. adolescents with positive relationships with their parents almost certainly pay closer attention to the way their parents act.

9. The implied main idea of paragraph 2 is that
   A. substance use or nonuse is dependent on an adolescent's relationship with his or her parents.
   B. adolescents who had negative relationships with their parents did not model the parent's use of alcohol or drugs.
   C. adolescents whose parents use drugs or alcohol may or may not copy their parents.
   D. adolescents who had negative relationships with their parents who use drugs or alcohol are better off.

10. The implied idea of paragraph 3 is that
    A. people are influenced by those who are attractive.
    B. behaviors you have observed become memories that will later influence your behavior.
    C. observational learning affects an individual on three levels.
    D. you will learn from someone you want to pay attention to.

2
Details of Support

This section tests your ability to recognize details that support the main idea of a passage or paragraph. You must be able to distinguish details that support the main idea from *general*, *irrelevant*, or *inaccurate* details.

Basically, supporting details must all relate to the main idea either directly through *primary* details or indirectly through *secondary* details (statements that explain or support primary details). Therefore, effective writing usually moves from *general* statements to *specific, concrete supports*. Details answer the classical questions: how, who, what when where, and why. A general statement needs additional information to answer these same questions. Use the **RECAPS** test to identify statements of supporting details:

- **R**easons
- **E**xamples
- **C**haracteristics
- **A**nalysis and explanations
- **P**eople and places
- **S**enses (sight, sound, smell, taste, touch)

- Consider the following example passage from the first section. Notice the application of **RECAPS** to identify the types of details that support the underlined topic sentence. Remember, supports are of two kinds: primary or *major* (which directly support the main idea and secondary or *minor* (which explain the primary supporting details).

EXAMPLE: <u>Great transformations had taken place in Western society between the beginning of the sixteenth century and the end of the eighteenth.</u> Those transformations became evident in philosophical, economical, scientific, and political arenas. The *Reformation* had *shattered* the unity of Christendom, and the *Enlightenment* had *challenged* the *roots* of Christian belief itself (secondary support: **reasons and examples**). The *European economy* had acquired a *global dimension* through the *conquest* and *exploitation* of the *New World* and the *expansion* of its markets in *Asia* and *Africa* (secondary support: **examples, explanation, and places**). The *scientific revolution* had *reordered* Western people's *views* of the *cosmos* and themselves (secondary support: **example**). Yet the political order of Europe had remained static (contrasting primary support). The *nations* of Europe were still *governed* by *monarchs* and *princes* (secondary support: **characteristics**). The *nobility* was still *predominant*; its *privileges* seemingly more *entrenched* than ever (secondary support: **characteristics**).

The French Revolution challenged all that (primary support: **example**). Within a matter of weeks in the summer of *1789*, a social and political *edifice* that had stood for *1,000 years* was *torn down*, and for a generation all of Europe was caught up in the *convulsive changes* that ensued (secondary support: **places, dates, numbers, and explanation**). From the very beginning, the revolution was recognized as the most important event of the age (secondary support: **characteristic**). In its *turmoil* and *agony* the *shape* of the modern world first *became visible* (secondary support: **characteristic**). (Greaves, Richard L., Robert Zaller, and Jennifer Tolbert Roberts. 1992. *Civilizations of the West: The Human Adventure: Volume C, From the French Revolution to the Present.* 597-598)

- Take an additional look at how these details look in an outline form. Many times, an outline helps to make visible the relationship between general and specific details.

<u>Main Idea</u>: Great transformations had taken place in Western society between the beginning of the sixteenth century and the end of the eighteenth.

    I.   Those transformations became evident in philosophical, economical, scientific areas. (primary support: statement of clarification).

        A.   The *Reformation* had *shattered* the unity of Christendom, and the *Enlightenment* had *challenged* the *roots* of Christian belief itself (secondary support: **reasons and examples**).

        B.   The *European economy* had acquired a *global dimension* through the *conquest* and *exploitation* of the *New World* and the *expansion* of its markets in *Asia* and *Africa* (secondary support: **examples, explanation, and places**).

        C.   The *scientific revolution* had *reordered* Western people's *views* of the *cosmos* and themselves (secondary support: **example**).

        D.   Yet the political order of Europe had remained static (contrasting primary support: transition idea).

            1.   The *nations* of Europe were still *governed* by *monarchs* and *princes* (secondary support: **characteristics**).

            2.   The *nobility* was still *predominant*; its *privileges* seemingly more *entrenched* than ever (secondary support: **characteristics**).

    II.   *The French Revolution challenged* all that (primary support: **example**).

        A.   Within a matter of weeks in the summer of *1789*, a social and political *edifice* that had stood for *1,000 years* was *torn down*, and for a generation all of Europe was caught up in the *convulsive changes* that ensued (secondary support: **places, dates, numbers, and explanation)**.

        B.   From the very beginning, the revolution was recognized as the most important event of the age (secondary support: **characteristic**).

        C.   In its *turmoil* and *agony* the *shape* of the modern world first *became visible* (secondary support: **characteristic**).

Exercises: Details of Support

PASSAGE #1
Read the passage below and answer the following questions.

1   Do you believe that your Zodiac sign matters? So many people, apparently do that the home page for the *Yahoo!* site on the World Wide Web will automatically provide your daily horoscope. But astrology—along with palm reading and tea-leaf reading, and all their relatives—is not a branch of psychology; it is pseudopsychology. Pseudopsychology

5   is superstition or unsupported opinion pretending to be science. Pseudopsychology is not just "bad psychology," which rests on poorly documented observations or badly designed studies and, therefore, has questionable foundations. Pseudopsychology is not psychology at all. It may look and sound like psychology, but it is not science.

    Appearances can be misleading. Consider extrasensory perception (ESP). Is this

10   pseudopsychology? ESP refers to a collection of mental abilities that do not rely on the ordinary senses or abilities. Telepathy, for instance, is the ability to read minds. This sounds not only wonderful but magical. No wonder people are fascinated by the possibility that they, too, may have latent, untapped, extraordinary abilities. The evidence that such abilities really exist is shaky. But the mere fact that many experiments on ESP

15   have come up empty does not mean that the experiments themselves are bad or "unscientific." One can conduct a perfectly good experiment, guarding against bias and expectancy of effects, even on ESP. Such research is not necessarily pseudopsychology.

    Let's say you wanted to study telepathy. You might arrange to test pairs of participants, with one member of each pair acting as "sender" and the other as "receiver." Both the

20   sender and receiver would look at hands of playing cards that contained the same four cards. The sender would focus on one card (say, an ace), and would "send" the receiver a mental image of the chosen card. The receiver's job would be to guess which card the sender is seeing. By chance alone, with only four cards to choose from, the receiver would guess right about 25% of the time. So the question is, can the receiver do better

25   than mere guesswork? In this study, you would measure the percentage of times the receiver picks the right card, and compare this to what you would expect from guessing alone.

    However, what if the sender provided visible clues (accidentally or on purpose) that have nothing to do with ESP, perhaps smiling when "sending" an ace, grimacing when

30   "sending" a two. A better experiment would have sender and receiver in different rooms, thus controlling for such possible problems. Furthermore, what if people have an unconscious bias to prefer red over black cards, which leads both sender and receiver to select them more often than would be dictated by chance? This difficulty can be countered by including a control condition, in which a receiver guesses cards when the

35   sender is not actually sending. Whether ESP can be considered a valid, reliable phenomenon will depend on the results of such studies. If they conclusively show that there is nothing to it, then people who claim to have ESP or to understand it will be trying to sell a bill of goods—and will be engaging in pseudopsychology. But as long as proper studies are under way, we cannot dismiss them as pseudopsychology. (Kosslyn, Stephen M., and Robin S. Rosenberg. *Psychology.* 2nd ed. Boston: Allyn and Bacon, 2004)

1. According to the passage, ESP
   A. is a pseudopsychology.
   B. has not as yet been proved or disproved.
   C. is related to astrology and palm reading.
   D. is an ability that everyone can learn to draw on.

2. According to paragraph 1, pseudopsychology is
   A. a branch of psychology.
   B. a science.
   C. a badly designed study.
   D. a superstition.

3. Research experiments on telepathy
   A. must guard against bias.
   B. are difficult to set up.
   C. have shown that telepathy is largely guesswork.
   D. is a waste of time.

4. According to paragraph 4, a better experiment would
   A. eliminate guesswork.
   B. eliminate problems of visible clues and unconscious bias.
   C. use playing cards.
   D. measure the percentage of times the receiver picks the right card.

PASSAGE 2
Read the passage below and answer the following questions.

1   North America has ten species of skunks. The one most people have seen—or at least
smelled—is the abundant and widespread striped skunk. Another species is the spotted
skunk, rarely seen but especially interesting because it illustrates some important
concepts about biological species. This particular skunk belongs to a species called the
5   western spotted skunk. The adult is only about the size of a house cat, but it has a potent
chemical arsenal that makes up for its small size. Before spraying her potent musk, a
female guarding her young usually warns an intruder by raising her tail, stamping her
forefeet, raking the ground with her claws, or even doing a handstand. When all else fails,
she can spray her penetrating odor for three meters with considerable accuracy.

10   The western spotted skunk inhabits a variety of environments in the United States, from
the Pacific coast to the western Great Plains. It is closely related to the eastern spotted
skunk, which occurs throughout the southeastern and midwestern United States. The
ranges of these two species overlap, and the two species look so much alike that even
experts can have a difficult time telling them apart. Both are black with broken white
15   stripes and spots. Individuals of the western species are, on average, slightly smaller, and
some have a white tip on the tail, but these and other minor differences in body form are
not always present.

For many years, biologists debated whether all spotted skunks belong to one species. But in the 1960s, studies of sexual reproduction in these animals showed that they are indeed

20   two species. Reproduction in the eastern spotted skunk is a straightforward affair. Mating occurs in late winter, and young are born between April and July. In marked contrast, the western spotted skunk includes what is called delayed development in its reproductive cycle. Mating takes place in the later summer and early fall, and zygotes begin to develop in the uterus of the female. Further development, however, is temporarily stopped at an

25   early point called the blastocyst stage. Blastocysts remain dormant in the female's uterus throughout the winter months and resume growth in the spring, with the young (usually 5-7) being born in May or June. Because mating occurs at different times of the year for the two species, there is no opportunity for gene flow between populations of eastern and western spotted skunks. Thus, they are separate species, despite the pronounced

30   similarities in their body form and coloration.

Spotted skunks show us that looks can be deceiving. Without knowledge of the mating cycles, we could interpret the minor differences between the two species as insignificant and conclude that there is only one species of spotted skunk in North America. (Adapted from Campbell, Neil A., Lawrence G. Mitchell, and Jane B. Reece. *Biology*. 3rd ed. San Francisco: Benjamin Cummings, 2000)

5.   The western spotted skunk and the eastern spotted skunk
       A. are about the size of a house cat.
       B. are not difficult to tell apart.
       C. live in completely different parts of the United States.
       D. belong to the same species.

6.   The female western spotted skunk guarding her young warns an intruder by
       A. hissing.
       B. running in circles.
       C. stamping her forefeet.
       D. swishing her tail.

7.   Biologists discovered that the two skunks were different species by studying their
       A. migration patterns.
       B. range overlap.
       C. chemical composition of their potent musk sprays.
       D. mating habits.

8.   The western spotted skunk's reproductive cycle
       A. occurs in late winter.
       B. occurs at the same time as the eastern spotted skunk.
       C. includes delayed development.
       D. takes longer than the eastern spotted skunk.

9.   The eastern and western spotted skunks are interesting because
       A. they live in a variety of environments across the U.S.
       B. they illustrate some important concepts about biological species.
       C. they could become extinct.

10. The most important discovery about the North American eastern and western spotted skunk is that
    A. their habitats overlap.
    B. there is more than one species of spotted skunk.
    C. they are difficult to tell apart.
    D. they defend their young similarly.

3
Purpose of Passage

This section tests your ability to identify the author's main stated or implied purpose in a passage or paragraph. You must be able to distinguish between the different types of purposes: to inform, to persuade, to entertain, to describe, to narrate, to evaluate, to praise, to criticize, to analyze, to inspire, to clarify, to illustrate, and to define. You must also be able to distinguish between **primary** and **secondary purposes.**

Sometimes an author may find it necessary to combine purposes. For example, the purposes to entertain and to illustrate can combine to create a humorous approach to teach an important lesson. Even when multiple purposes are used, one will dominate as the primary purpose.

A closely related skill is the ability to identify *tone*, the emotional mood created by use of language. Understanding the writer's tone of voice will help you understand the purpose of the passage. Purpose and tone are established with word choice. Authors choose words that are either objective, factual, or subjective, which expresses opinion or emotions.

EXAMPLES:

Purpose	Possible Tone	Possible Word Choice
To inform	instructional	objective, unbiased
To persuade	inspirational, convincing, shocking, insistent	subjective, emotional
To entertain	humorous	subjective, emotional
To describe	nostalgic, honest, clinical, graphic	subjective, emotional

Exercises: Purpose of Passage

PASSAGE #1
Read the following passage, and answer the question that follows.

1   Fungi have a number of practical uses for humans. Most of us have eaten mushrooms although we may not have realized that we were ingesting the fruiting bodies of subterranean fungi. In addition, mushrooms are not the only fungi we eat. The distinctive flavors of certain kinds of cheeses, including Roquefort and blue cheese come from the
5   fungi used to ripen them. Highly prized gourmets are truffles, the fruiting bodies of certain mycorrhizal fungi associated with tree roots. The unicellular fungi, the yeasts, are important in food production. Yeasts are used in baking, brewing, and winemaking. Fungi are medically valuable as well. Some fungi produce antibiotics that are used to treat bacterial diseases. In fact, the first antibiotic discovered was penicillin, which is
10   made by the common mold called *Penicillium*. (Adapted fromCampbell, Neil A., Lawrence G. Mitchell, and Jane B. Reece. *Biology*. 3rd ed. San Francisco: Benjamin Cummings, 2000)

1.   The primary purpose of the above passage is to
     A. describe foods that are fungi.
     B. explain how fungi are used to ripen cheeses.
     C. gives examples of the uses of fungi.
     D. analyzes the medical and nutritional benefits of fungi.

PASSAGE #2
Read the following passage, and answer the question that follows.

1   John Castle's lifestyle gives us a glimpse into how the super-rich live. After earning a degree in physics at MIT and an MBA at Harvard, John went into banking and securities, where he made more than $100 million.

      Wanting to be close to someone famous, John bought President John F. Kennedy's
5   "Winter White House," an oceanfront estate in Palm Beach, Florida. John spent $11 million to remodel the 13,000-square-foot house so it would be more to his liking. Among those changes: adding bathrooms numbers 14 and 15. He likes to show off John F. Kennedy's bed and also the dresser that has the drawer labeled "black underwear," carefully hand-lettered by Rose Kennedy.

10   If John gets bored at his beachfront estate—or tired of swimming in the Olympic-size pool where JFK swam the weekend before his assassination—he entertains himself by riding one of his thoroughbred horses at his nearby 10-acre ranch. If this fails to ease his boredom, he can relax aboard his custom-built, 45-foot Hinckley yacht.

      The yacht is a real source of diversion. He once boarded it for an around-the-world trip.
15   He didn't stay on board, though—just joined the cruise from time to time. A captain and crew kept the vessel sailing in the right direction, and whenever John felt like it, he would fly in and stay a few days. Then he would fly back to the States to direct his business. He

did this about a dozen times, flying perhaps 150,000 miles, an interesting way to get around the world.

20   How much does a custom-built Hinckley yacht cost? John can't tell you. As he says, "I don't want to know what anything costs. When you've got enough money, price doesn't make a difference. That's part of the freedom of being rich." (Adapted from Henslin, James M. *Sociology*. 6th ed. Boston: Allyn and Bacon, 2003)

2.   The primary purpose of the above passage is to
      A. persuade the reader that John Castle's lifestyle should be envied.
      B. describe John Castle's lifestyle as an example of how the super-rich live.
      C. criticize John Castle's squandering his money.
      D. inspire the reader to become wealthy.

PASSAGE #3
Read the following passage, and answer the question that follows.

1   The National Child Abuse Prevention and Treatment Act of 1974 defines child abuse and neglect as "physical or mental injury, sexual abuse or exploitation, negligent treatment, or maltreatment of a child under the age of eighteen or the age specified under the child protection law of the state in question, by a person who is responsible for the child's
5   welfare, under circumstances which indicate that the child's health or welfare is harmed or threatened thereby."

      The laws of every state require teachers to report suspected cases of child abuse and neglect. Every state grants teachers who make such reports immunity from civil and criminal suits. State laws vary in their requirements, and teachers should become familiar
10   with the laws where they teach. Most states require an oral report to an administrator followed by a written statement. The law will protect teachers who act in good faith. Teachers should not hesitate to file a report if they believe a student is a victim of abuse or neglect. In most states teachers can be fined or imprisoned if they do *not* make the report, and in some states they can be sued for neglect.

15   A teacher who sees a student exhibit indicators of child abuse and neglect over a period of time should think seriously about why the indicators are present. As in other areas of the law, the *reasonable person* standard applies: Under similar circumstances, would a reasonable person suspect abuse or neglect? If your answer is yes, you should make a report. Remember, the law will protect you if you act in good faith. Do not be blind to the
20   problem. (Adapted from Newman, Joseph W. *America's Teachers*. 4th ed. Boston: Allyn and Bacon, 2002)

3.   The author's primary purpose in the above passage is to
      A. define child abuse to teachers.
      B. explain state laws regarding child abuse to teachers.
      C. inform teachers about child abuse indicators.
      D. convince teachers that it is their duty to report child abuse.

PASSAGE #4
Read the following passage, and answer the question that follows.

1   There are vast cultural differences in what is considered proper when it comes to criticism. In some cultures, being kind to the person is more important than telling the absolute truth and so members may say things that are complimentary, but untrue, in a logical sense. Those who come from cultures that are highly individual and competitive,
5   such as the United States, Germany, and Sweden, may find public criticism a normal part of the learning process. Those who come from cultures that are more collectivist and that emphasize the group rather than the individual, such as Japan, Mexico, and Korea, are likely to find giving and receiving public criticism uncomfortable. Thus, people from individual cultures may readily criticize others and are likely to expect the same
10   "courtesy" from other listeners. After all, this person might reason, "If I'm going to criticize your skills to help you improve, I expect you to help me in the same way." Persons from collectivist cultures, on the other hand, may feel that it's more important to be polite and courteous than to help someone learn a skill. Cultural rules to maintain peaceful relations among the Japanese and politeness among many Asian cultures may
15   conflict with the Western classroom cultural norm to voice criticism.

       The difficulties are compounded when you interpret unexpected behavior through your own cultural filters. For example, if a speaker who expects comments and criticism gets none, he or she may interpret the silence to mean that the audience didn't care or wasn't listening. But they may have been listening very intently. They may simply be operating
20   with a different cultural rule—a rule that says it's impolite to criticize or evaluate another person's work, especially in public. (Adapted from DeVito, Joseph A. *Essentials of Human Communication*. 3rd ed. New York: Longman, 1999)

4.   The main purpose of the above passage is to
       A. contrast cultural differences in public criticism.
       B. explain how to criticize effectively.
       C. persuade the reader to respect cultural differences.
       D. describe the effects of cultural miscommunications.

PASSAGE #5
Read the following passage, and answer the question that follows.

1   Although many people think of First Ladies as well-dressed homemakers presiding over White House dinners, there is much more to the job. The First Lady has no official government position. Yet she is often at the center of national attention. The media chronicles every word she speaks and every hairstyle she adopts.

5   Abigail Adams (an early feminist) and Dolly Madison counseled and lobbied their husbands. Edith Galt Wilson was the most powerful First lady, virtually running the government when her husband, Woodrow, suffered a paralyzing stroke in 1919. Eleanor Roosevelt wrote a nationally syndicated newspaper column and tirelessly traveled and advocated New Deal policies. She became her crippled husband's eyes and ears around

10   the country and urged him to adopt liberal social welfare policies. Lady Bird Johnson chose to focus on one issue, beautification, and most of her successors followed this pattern. Rosalyn Carter chose mental health, Nancy Reagan selected drugs, and Barbara Bush picked literacy.

In what was perhaps a natural evolution in a society where women have moved into
15   positions formerly held only by males, Hillary Rodham Clinton attained the most responsible and visible leadership position ever held by a First Lady. She had been an influential advisor to the President, playing an active role in the selection of nominees for cabinet and judicial posts, for example. Most publicly, she headed the planning for the President's massive health care reform plan in 1993 and became, along with her husband,
20   its primary advocate. (Adapted from Edwards, George C., Martin P. Wattenberg, and Robert L. Lineberry. *Government in America*. 9th ed. New York: Longman, 2000)

5.   The main purpose of the above passage is to
    A. contrast the activities of the First Ladies.
    B. explain the way the First Lady does her job.
    C. convince the reader that First Ladies are feminists.
    D. illustrate the public roles of the First Ladies.

PASSAGE #6
Read the following passage, and answer the question that follows.

1   President Truman's decision to order the atomic bombings on the Japanese cities of Hiroshima and Nagasaki has been the subject of intense historical debate. Truman's defenders argue that the bombs ended the war quickly, avoiding the necessity of a costly invasion and the probable loss of tens of thousands of Americans' lives and hundreds of
5   Japanese lives. According to some intelligence estimates, an invasion might have cost 268,000 American casualties, with Japanese costs several times that figure.

Truman's defenders also argue that Hiroshima and Nagasaki were legitimate targets with both military bases and war industry, and their civilian populations had been showered with leaflets warning them to evacuate. Finally, they argue that two bombs were
10   ultimately necessary to end the war. They note that even after the atomic bomb had fallen on Hiroshima, the Japanese war minister implored the nation's Supreme Council "for one last great battle on Japanese soil—as demanded by the national honor. . . . Would it not be wondrous for this whole nation to be destroyed like a beautiful flower."

Truman's critics argue that the war might have ended even without the atomic bombings.
15   They maintain that the Japanese economy would have been strangled by a continued naval blockade and forced to surrender by conventional firebombing. The revisionists also contend that the President had options apart from using the bombs. They believe that it might have been possible to induce a Japanese surrender by a demonstration of the atomic bomb's power or by providing a more specific warning of the damage it could
20   produce or by guaranteeing the emperor's position in postwar Japan.

The revisionists also believe that estimates of potential American casualties were grossly inflated after the war to justify the bombing. Finally, they argue that the bomb might have

been dropped mainly to justify its cost or to scare the Soviet Union. The Soviet Union entered the Japanese war August 8, and some revisionists charge that the bombings were
25   designed to end the war before the Red army could occupy northern China. (Adapted from Martin, James Kirby et al. *America and Its Peoples*. 5th ed. New York: Longman, 2004)

6.   The authors' purpose in the above passage is to
      A. describe the effects of the U. S. dropping the atomic bombs on the Japanese.
      B. inform the reader of the reasons for dropping the atomic bombs on Hiroshima and Nagasaki.
      C. persuade the reader that the dropping of atomic bombs on Hiroshima and Nagasaki was wrong.
      D. present the two sides of the debate over the dropping of the atomic bombs on Hiroshima and Nagasaki.

PASSAGE #7
Read the following passage, and answer the question that follows.

1   A single parent may experience a variety of problems. First of all, it may be difficult to meet the emotional needs of the child. There are a variety of ways to express love for a child. Telling a child he or she is loved and demonstrating that love with quality time serve to express love; however, the demands of working and maintaining a home may be
5   so overwhelming that a child's emotional needs may not be met adequately. It also may be hard for the single parent to provide proper supervision for the child. Making arrangements for the child's care and supervision is difficult and costly and may take a large share of the budget. In addition, because women tend to make less money than men, households headed by women can experience financial difficulties. Finally, the single
10   parent may experience unfulfilled emotional and sexual needs. Unmet emotional needs can develop because of the lack of time to seek a relationship. Because most single parents wish to hide their sexual involvement from their child, finding a time and place can present problems. Nevertheless, being a single parent does not have to be a disaster. It is important that single parents have sufficient financial, material, and emotional
15   support to meet their own and their child's demands. (Adapted from Anspaugh, David J., and Gene Ezell. *Teaching Today's Health*. 7th ed. San Francisco: Pearson, 2004)

7.   The authors' purpose in the above paragraph is to
      A. argue the disadvantages of single parenthood.
      B. explain the types of problems single parents have.
      C. convince the reader that children in single parent homes suffer.
      D. give the effects of divorce on children.

PASSAGE #8
Read the following passage, and answer the question that follows.

1   Many overweight and obese individuals are trying to lose weight. Although it took several months and years to put on the extra weight, many of them are looking for a quick way to lose that weight. This attitude results in choosing quick-weight-loss diets that are not effective and may be harmful.

5   Some choose metabolic products, such as herbs or caffeine, to lose weight. Herbs have not been shown to speed the loss of fat, and caffeine shows little promise as a weight-loss aid.

     Others go on very-low-calorie diets, which severely restrict nutrients and can result in serious metabolic imbalances. Weight can be lost on this type of diet; much of the weight
10   lost will be lean protein tissue and/or water, not fat. This results in harm to the muscles (including the heart), loss of essential vitamins and minerals through the water loss, and dizziness and fatigue. Further, if one cuts calories, this slows the metabolism; once this person goes off the diet, the metabolism remains slow and the body continues to use few calories—and the pounds come back.

15   Liquid protein diets operate on the theory that insulin is controlled and therefore more fat is burned. With this type of diet, ketosis will result. Ketosis will increase blood levels of uric acid, a risk factor for gout and kidney stones. There is not research evidence that carbohydrates lead to fat storage and weight; further, the excessive protein in this diet can damage the kidneys and cause osteoporosis.

20   Prescription drugs, such as Redux and Pondimin (fen-phen), curb hunger by increasing the level of serotonin in the brain. These were intended for the obese, but were banned in 1997 after the FDA found strong evidence that they could seriously damage the heart.

     Some people try crash diets to lose a moderate amount of weight in a very short period. These types of diets can damage several body systems, and have been proven not to work
25   because most of these individuals regain their weight. This yo-yo dieting causes many health problems and shortens lifespan. The best way to lose weight is to lose weight slowly (no more than one-half to one pound a week), eat properly and in moderation, and exercise. (Adapted from Anspaugh, David J., and Gene Ezell. *Teaching Today's Health.* 7th ed. San Francisco: Pearson, 2004)

8.   The main purpose of the above paragraph is to
     A. classify the types of quick diets that are ineffective and harmful.
     B. persuade the reader that crash diets are harmful.
     C. describe fad diets.
     D. explain the best way to lose weight.

PASSAGE #9
Read the following passage, and answer the question that follows.

1   The dramatic difference between the social status of the Egyptian nobility and that of the common people is reflected in their respective burial rites. The keen Egyptian interest in the afterlife, combined with strikingly materialistic criteria for happiness, made lavish tombs for the pharaohs (Egyptian rulers) seem particularly important. Elaborate goods
5   were buried with the pharaoh to assure him a gracious existence in the world beyond, and a processional causeway linked each pyramid to a temple constructed for the worship of the pharaoh; adjacent to the pyramid was a building to house the special cedar boat that

would carry him on his voyage to the land of the dead. The pyramid served as the core of an entire necropolis, or city of the dead, which included small pyramids for the wives and
10   daughters of the pharaoh and mastabas for the nobility. Even a minor royal official spent a considerable portion of his time preparing an elaborate tomb for his afterlife, and he would want his corpse to be mummified because of the Egyptian belief that the *ka*, the spirit of life in each person, periodically returned to the body. The corpse of an average farmer, however, was typically wrapped in a piece of linen and deposited in a cave or pit
15   with only a staff and a pair of sandals to facilitate the journey to the next world; some bodies were even left in the open sand of the desert. (Adapted from Greaves, Richard L., Robert Zaller, and Jennifer Tolbert Roberts. *Civilizations of the West*. 2nd ed. New York: Longman, 1997)

9.   The author's main purpose in the above passage is
      A. to explain the Egyptian belief in the afterlife.
      B. to give reasons for building pyramids for the pharaohs.
      C. to show the difference in burial rites according to social status.
      D. to describe the lavish tombs of the pharaohs.

PASSAGE #10
Read the following passage, and answer the question that follows.

1   "Street gangs" are a more formal variety of youth gang. They generally have leaders and a hierarchy of membership roles and responsibilities. They are named, and their members mark their identity with tattoos or "colors." While many street gangs are involved in violence, not all are. An anthropologist who did research among nearly forty street gangs
5   in New York, Los Angeles, and Boston learned much about why individuals join gangs, providing insights that contradict popular thinking on this subject.

One common stereotype is that young boys join gangs because they are from homes with no male authority figure with whom they could identify. This study showed that equal numbers of gang members were from intact nuclear households as from those with an
10   absent father. Another common perception is that the gang replaces a missing feeling of family as a motive. This study, again, showed that the same number of gang members reported having close family ties as those who did not.

Those who were gang members shared a personality type called a "defiant individualist." This type has five traits: intense competitiveness, mistrust or wariness, self-reliance,
15   social isolation, and a strong survival instinct. Poverty, especially urban poverty, leads to the development of this type of personality. Many of these youths want to be economically successful, but social conditions channel their interests and skills into illegal pursuits rather than into legal pathways of achievement. (Adapted from Miller, Barbara D. *Cultural Anthropology*. 2nd ed. Boston: Allyn and Bacon, 2002)

10.   The main purpose of the above paragraph is to
      A. discourage youths from joining a gang.
      B. argues that street gang members come from homes with no authority figure.
      C. gives reasons youths join street gangs.
      D. define the typical gang personality type.

CHAPTER 2: *STRUCTURAL SKILLS*

1
Organizational Patterns

This section tests your ability to identify the main organizational pattern in a passage or paragraph. You must recognize that details are structured to form organizational patterns. An **organizational pattern** is the **arrangement** of **details** into a **clear structure**.

The structure of details brings *coherence*, a *logical* flow of ideas based on the *relationship* of ideas to each other and to the *author's purpose*. For example, an author's main purpose may be to convince the reader of the need to have regular physical exams to prevent health problems before they can occur. To be convincing, the author may choose to explain the short and long-term effects of an untreated gum disease by using the cause and effect pattern of organization. Or the author may choose to contrast the story of an individual who has had regular exams to one who has not, using the point-to-point contrast pattern of organization.

This skill is also closely tied to the next two sections, for the organizational pattern is created through relationships between and within sentences. Each pattern of organization has a set of identification or *transition words* related to its meaning. These transitional words found in and between sentences convey the organizational pattern.

Patterns of organization and related words

• **Cause/effect:**	Accordingly, as a result, so, therefore, thus
• **Comparison:**	Likewise, in the same way, similarly.
• **Contrast:**	At the same time, but, conversely, however, in contrast, nevertheless, nonetheless, on the one hand, on the other hand, still, yet.
• **Classification:** (simple listing)	Category, class, collection, division, kind, group, type, set, sort.
• **Definition:**	Uses a combination of the other patterns to tell what a concept or term means and how it is different from other concepts or terms in its class.
• **Example/illustration:**	As an illustration, for example, for instance
• **Generalization/example:**	By and large, commonly, generally, usually,
• **Statement/clarification:**	Normally, namely, specifically, thus.
• **Process/narration/time order/listing:**	Afterward, before, later, first, second, third, next, then, finally, currently, meanwhile, subsequently, immediately, eventually, currently.
• **Spatial/description/place order:**	Above, below, adjacent, at the side, in the front, in the back, in the foreground, in the background, in the distance, here, there, North, South, East, West.

Exercises: Organizational Patterns

PASSAGE #1
Read the passage and answer the question that follows.

1   Regardless of the type of job you have, you have to divide your time between work and school. The following suggestions will help you balance these two segments of your life. First of all, make sure that your supervisor knows you are attending college and that your job helps pay for it. He or she may be more understanding and helpful if he or she knows

5   you are a serious student. In addition, try to find a coworker who may be willing to switch work hours or take your hours if you need extra time to study. Next, if possible, try to build a work schedule around your class schedule. For example, if you have an eight-o'clock class on Tuesday mornings, try not to work until midnight on Monday night. Finally, allow study time for each class. Make sure you have time between class

10   sessions to do homework and complete assigned readings. For example, if you have a Tuesday/Thursday class, make sure you have some study time between the two session. (Adapted from McWhorter, Kathleen T. *Study and Critical Thinking Skills in College.* 5th ed. New York: Longman, 2003)

1.   For this passage, the author uses an organizational pattern that
    A. summarizes the problems of a working student.
    B. gives reasons for attending school full-time instead of working and studying at the same time.
    C. discusses how to get along with your supervisor and coworkers.
    D. gives instructions on how to balance work and school time.

PASSAGE #2
Read the passage below and answer the question that follows.

1   Contrary to popular assumption, slavery was not usually based on racism, but on one of three other factors. The first was debt. In some cultures, an individual who could not pay a debt could be enslaved by the creditor. The second was crime. Instead of being killed, a murderer or thief might be enslaved by the family of the victim as compensation for their

5   loss. The third was war and conquest. When one group of people conquered another, they often enslaved some of the vanquished. Historian Gerda Lerner notes that the first people enslaved through warfare were women. When premodern men raided a village or camp, they killed the men, raped the women, and the brought the women back as slaves. The women were valued for sexual purposes, for reproduction, and for their labor. (Henslin, James M. *Sociology.* 6th ed. Boston: Allyn and Bacon, 2003)

2.   For this passage, the author uses an organizational pattern that
    A. describes what happened to women after warfare in premodern times.
    B. explains the reasons for slavery.
    C. contrasts premodern and modern forms of slavery.
    D. defines slavery.

PASSAGE #3
Read the passage below and answer the question that follows.

1   Cyberliteracy is not purely a print literacy, nor is Internet literacy purely an oral literacy. Cyberliteracy is an electronic literacy—newly emerging in a new medium—that combines features of both print and the spoken word, and the medium does so in ways that change how we read, speak, think, and interact with others. Once we see that online texts

5   are not exactly written or spoken, we begin to understand that cyberliteracy requires a special form of critical thinking. Communication in the online world is not quite like anything else. Written messages, such as letters (even when written on a computer), are usually created slowly and with reflection, allowing the writer to think and revise even as the document is chugging away at the printer. But electronic *discourse*—talking,

10   conversing, interacting—encourages us to reply quickly, often in a more oral style. In discourse, we blur the normally accepted distinctions, such as writing versus speaking, and conventions, such as punctuation and spelling. Normal rules about writing, editing, and revising a document do not make much sense in this environment. (Adapted from Shedletsky, Leonard J., and Joan E. Aitken. *Human Communication on the Internet.* Boston: Allyn and Bacon, 2004)

3.   For this passage, the author uses an organizational pattern that
   A. defines cyberliteracy.
   B. shows similarities between online and written communication.
   C. describes critical thinking.
   D. explains how to become cyberliterate.

PASSAGE #4
Read the passage below and answer the questions that follow.

1   The most boisterous forms of entertainment in the Roman Empire involved the excitement of a roaring crowd. The huge seating capacity of the Circus Maximus, which could probably accommodate a quarter of a million spectators, made chariot races an extremely popular diversion in the city of Rome. Bets were placed both on and off the

5   track, and the seating regulations of the Colosseum, which separated the sexes, did not operate in the Circus, where men and women sat together, heightening the tension and festivity of the atmosphere. An element of danger also contributed to the air of excitement, as ancient chariot races afforded the same kinds of entertaining and often fatal crashes that are common to automobile competitions today. But the tumult of the

10   races was tame in comparison to the spectacles offered in the amphitheaters of the empire, where emperors, local officials, and public-minded citizens vied with one another to give the most memorable shows.

   Sadism and voyeurism were key elements in Roman entertainment. Savage gladiatorial combats to the death and the feeding of humans to wild beasts are not inventions of

15   Hollywood; they were a staple of Roman entertainment. Most residents of the empire who lived anywhere near a city saw a number of people killed in the arena over their lifetimes. Nearly all would have been mystified by the anxieties people feel today about the make-believe violence in the movies and on television, and the ghoulish curiosity

about witnessing bloody deaths that people try to suppress and deny in our own society seems to have caused the Romans no embarrassment. Uninhibitedly, they flocked in great numbers to the arenas of doom. (Adapted from Greaves, Richard L., Robert Zaller, and Jennifer Tolbert Roberts. *Civilizations of the West*. New York: Longman, 1997)

4. For this passage, the author uses an overall organizational pattern that
    A. gives the effects of violent entertainment on the Roman people.
    B. explains how gladiators fought in the arena.
    C. gives examples of the forms of entertainment that excited the Romans.
    D. analyzes the reasons Romans enjoyed sadism and voyeurism.

5. The second paragraph is organized by
    A. contrasting the Roman's acceptance of violence to our anxiety about seeing violence in movies and television.
    B. defining sadism.
    C. explaining the key elements of Roman entertainment: sadism and voyeurism.
    D. describing Hollywood gladiator movies.

PASSAGE #5
Read the passage below and answer the question that follows.

1   Nonflowing bodies of water such as lakes become contaminated in stages. First, pollutants such as animal fertilizer, detergents, industrial waste, and sewage are dumped into the water supply. As a result, an accelerated growth of algae occurs. As algae growth skyrockets on a diet of inorganic pollutants, especially nitrogen and phosphorus, a
5   blanket of slime covers the water. Eventual death of the algae results in bacterial decomposition that consumes the oxygen present. This oxygen deficit kills fish and other lake inhabitants, many of which are valuable as food resources, and as recently suggested, disrupts freshwater animals' endocrine systems. Eventually, the body of water becomes contaminated beyond use. (Adapted from Anspaugh, David J., and Gene Ezell. *Teaching Today's Health*. 7th ed. San Francisco: Benjamin Cummings, 2004)

6. This paragraph is organized by
    A. listing the types of chemicals that pollute our water.
    B. describing the growth of algae.
    C. defining water pollution.
    D. explaining the process of water contamination.

PASSAGE #6
Read the passage below and answer the questions that follow.

1   One type of anxiety disorder is the panic disorder. The hallmark of panic disorder is the experience of panic attacks, episodes of intense fear or discomfort accompanied by symptoms such as palpitations, breathing difficulties, chest pain, nausea, sweating, dizziness, fear of going crazy or doing something uncontrollable, fear of impending
5   doom, and a sense of unreality. Symptoms reach their peak within a few minutes of the beginning of an attack, which can last from minutes to hours. Often these attacks are not associated with a specific situation or object and may even seem to occur randomly. One

study of college students found that 12% of the participants experienced spontaneous panic attacks during their lifetimes. Some people may have episodes of panic attacks, with years of remission; others may have more persistent symptoms.

People with panic disorder worry constantly about having more attacks, and in their attempts to avoid or minimize panic attacks, they may change their behavior. People may go to great lengths to try to avoid panic attacks, quitting their jobs, avoiding places (such as hot, crowded rooms or events) or activities that increase their heart rate (such as exercise or watching suspenseful movies or sporting events). Some people fear or avoid places that might be difficult to leave should a panic attack occur—for example, a plane or car. They may avoid leaving home or do so only with a close friend or relative. Such fear and avoidance can lead to agoraphobia, a condition in which the avoidance of places or activities restricts daily life. In some cases, people have agoraphobia without panic attacks, avoiding many places because they fear either losing control of themselves in some way (such as losing bladder control) or the fear the occurrence of less severe but still distressing panic symptoms. (Kosslyn, Stephen M., and Robin S. Rosenberg. *Psychology*. 2nd ed. Boston: Allyn and Bacon, 2004)

7. For this passage, the author uses the overall organizational pattern that
    A. contrasts panic attacks with agoraphobia.
    B. explains one type of disorder, panic disorder.
    C. explains recommended strategies for dealing with panic attacks.
    D. classifies the causes of panic attacks.

8. The second passage is organized by
    A. giving examples of things people do to avoid or minimize panic attacks.
    B. defining panic disorder.
    C. giving the steps for treatment.
    D. comparing types of panic avoidance behavior.

PASSAGE #7
Read the passage below and answer the questions that follow.

1   Plagiarism is using someone else's words and ideas without giving that person proper credit. Even when your use of a source may be perfectly legal, you may still be violating ethical standards if you do not give credit to the information source.

    Assume, for example, that you are writing a class report on genetically modified foods. In your research, you discover a very good paper on the Web. You decide that parts of this paper would complement your report quite nicely. Under copyright and fair use guidelines, you can reproduce portions of this paper without permission. But does this legal standard mean that you can use someone else's material freely, without giving that person credit? Even though it might be legal under fair use guidelines to reprint the material without notifying the copyright holder, using someone else's material or ideas without giving them credit is plagiarism.

Plagiarism is a serious infraction in most settings. Students can be suspended or expelled from school. Researchers can lose their jobs and their standing in the academic community. Most importantly, plagiarism is serious because it violates several of the

15   reasonable criteria for ethical decision making. Plagiarism violates your obligation to yourself to be truthful, and it violates your obligation to society to produce fair and accurate information. It also violates your obligation to other students and researchers. (Adapted from Gurak, Laura J., and John M. Lannon. *A Concise Guide to Technical Communication*. New York: Longman, 2001)

9.   For this passage, the author uses the overall organizational pattern that
    A. analyzes a situation in which plagiarism occurs.
    B. lists types of plagiarism.
    C. defines plagiarism.
    D. tells how to use information from the Web.

10.   The third paragraph is organized by
    A. describing the effects of plagiarism on students.
    B. defining ethical decision making.
    C. contrasting plagiarism at college and at work.
    D. giving reasons that plagiarism is a serious infraction.

PASSAGE #8
Read the passage below and answer the questions that follow.

1   During the seventeenth and eighteenth centuries, the process of childbirth in colonial America was conducted by women. The typical woman gave birth to her children at home, while female relatives and neighbors clustered at her bedside to offer support and encouragement.

5   Most women were assisted in childbirth not by a doctor but by a midwife. Most midwives were older women who relied on practical experience in delivering children. One midwife, Martha Ballard, who practiced in Augusta, Maine, delivered 996 babies with only 4 recorded fatalities. Skilled midwives were highly valued. Communities tried to attract experienced midwives by offering a salary or a rent-free house. In addition to

10   assisting in childbirth, midwives helped deliver the offspring of animals, attended the baptisms and burials of infants, and testified in court cases of illegitimate babies.

During labor, midwives administered no painkillers, except for alcohol. Pain in childbirth was considered God's punishment for Eve's sin of eating the forbidden fruit in the Garden of Eden. Women were merely advised to have patience, to pray, and during

15   labor, to restrain their groans and cries which upset the people near them.

After delivery, new mothers were often treated to a banquet. At one such event, visitors feasted on boiled pork, beef, poultry, roast beef, turkey pie, and tarts. Women from well-to-do families were then expected to spend three to four weeks in bed convalescing. Their attendants kept the fireplace burning and wrapped them in a heavy blanket in order to help them sweat out "poisons." Women from poorer families were generally back at work in one or two days. (Adapted from Martin, James Kirby, et al. *America and Its Peoples*. New York: Longman, 2004)

11. For this passage, the author uses the overall organizational pattern that
    A. gives religious reasons for pain in childbirth.
    B. illustrates the ways in which women assisted childbirth.
    C. explains the differences between childbirth for the rich and poor women.
    D. describes the dangers of childbirth.

12. The second paragraph is organized by
    A. describing midwives.
    B. arguing the advantages of midwives over doctors.
    C. listing the achievements of Martha Ballard.
    D. explaining how the midwife assists in childbirth.

PASSAGE #9
Read the passage below and answer the question that follows.

1   Deborah Tannen, sociologist and author, explains the differences in the listening behavior of men and women. Women seek to build rapport and establish a closer relationship and so they use listening to achieve these ends. For example, women use more listening cues that let the other person know they are paying attention and are interested. On the other hand,

5   men not only use fewer listening cues but interrupt more and will often change the topic to one they know more about or one that is less relational or people-oriented to one that is more factual, for example, sports, statistics, economic developments, or political problems. Men, research shows, play up their expertise, emphasize it, and use it to dominate the conversation. Women play down their expertise.

10   Research shows that men communicate with women in the same way they do with other men. Men are not showing disrespect for their female conversational partners, but are simply communicating as they normally do. Women, too, communicate as they do not only with men but also with other women.

     Tannen argues that the goal of a man in conversation is to be accorded respect, and so he

15   seeks to display his knowledge and expertise even if he has to change the topic from one he knows little about to one he knows a great deal about. A woman, on the other hand, seeks to be liked, and so she expresses agreement and less frequently interrupts to take her turn as speaker.

     Men and women also show that they are listening in different ways. A woman is more apt

20   to give lots of listening cues, such as interjecting, "yeah, uh-uh," nodding in agreement, and smiling. A man is more likely to listen quietly, without giving lots of listening cues as feedback. Tannen also argues, however, that men do listen less to women than women listen to men. The reason is that listening places the person in an inferior position whereas speaking places the person in a superior position.

25   There is no evidence to show that these differences represent any negative motives on the part of men to prove themselves superior or of women to ingratiate themselves. Rather, these differences in listening are largely the result of the way in which men and women have been socialized. (Adapted from DeVito, Joseph A. *Essentials of Human Communication*. 3rd ed. New York: Longman, 1999)

13.   For this passage, the author uses the overall organizational pattern that
       A. illustrates conversational behaviors of men and women.
       B. argues that men need to prove themselves superior when in conversation.
       C. contrasts the ways men and women listen.
       D. discusses the negative effects of male listening behavior on women.

14.   The first paragraph is organized by
       A. offering examples of how men do not listen to women.
       B. contrasting the listening cues used by men and women.
       C. explaining how women use listening to get close to a person.
       D. developing the theory that men do not disrespect female conversational patterns.

STUDY HINT:

The following section of exercises pulls some of its passages that you have already seen in one or more of the previous sections. The purpose of presenting you with the same passages in different sections is two-fold. First, the repetition imitates the state exit exam, which presents you with a passage and then asks you several different types of questions based on that one passage. These sets of questions address different skills. For example, one passage may have the questions about the following skills: main idea, relevance of supporting details, author's purpose, types of organization, word meaning in context.

The state exit test's use of one passage for several questions is the second reason for working with the same passages throughout the workbook. Many of these skills are connected to each other. For example, the author's purpose is closely connected to the pattern of organization and reinforced by tone. So it is important for you to see how one passage uses each of these skills for an overall effect. Study smart; compare these questions to the other sections where the passages also appear, and think about the relationship between the skills.

PASSAGE #10
Read the passage below and answer the question that follows.

1   On April 20, 1999, a school shooting of such immense proportions occurred which radically, if not permanently, altered public thinking and debate about student safety and security. After months of planning and preparation, 18-year-old Eric Harris and 17-year-old Dylan Klebold armed themselves with guns and explosives and headed off to
5   Columbine High School in Littleton, Colorado, to celebrate Adolph Hitler's birthday in a manner fitting their hero. By the time the assault ended with self-inflicted fatal gunshots, a dozen students and one teacher lay dead.

      In understanding the horrific actions of schoolyard snipers, it is as important to examine friendships as it is to delve into family background. At Columbine, Harris and Klebold

10   were generally seen as geeks or nerds, from the point of view of any of the large student cliques—the jocks, the punks, etc. Though excluded from mainstream student culture, they banded together and bonded together with several of their fellow outcasts in what they came to call the "Trench Coat Mafia." The image they attempted to create was clearly one of power and dominance—the barbaric incivility, the forces of darkness, the

15   preoccupation with Hitler, the celebration of evil and villainy. Harris and Klebold desperately wanted to feel important; and in the preparations they made to murder their classmates, the two shooters got their wish. For more than a year, they plotted and planned, colluded and conspired to put one over on their schoolmates, teachers, and parents. They amassed an arsenal of weapons, strategized about logistics, and made final

20   preparations—yet, until it was too late, not a single adult got wind of what Harris and Klebold intended to do.

    Birds of a feather may kill together. Harris, the leader, would likely have enjoyed the respect and admiration from Klebold, who in turn would have felt uplifted by the praise he received from his revered buddy. In their relationship, the two boys got from one

25   another what was otherwise missing from their lives—they felt special, they gained a sense of belonging, they were united against the world. As Harris remarked, as he and his friend made last-minute preparations to commit mass murder: "This is just a two-man war against everything else." (Adapted from Fox, James Alan, and Jack Levin. *The Will to Kill*. Boston: Allyn and Bacon, 2001)

15.   For this passage, the author uses the overall organizational pattern that
     A. describes the Columbine High School massacre.
     B. lists the effects of the Columbine High School massacre.
     C. tells the process Harris and Klebold used to prepare for the shootings.
     D. analyzes Harris and Klebold's friendship to understand their crime.

PASSAGE #11
Read the passage below and answer the question that follows.

1   Each of the 2000 or so species of firefly has its own way to signal a mate. When a female sees flashes of light from a male of her species, she reacts with flashes of her own. If the male sees her flashes, he automatically gives another display and flies in the female's direction. Members of both sexes are responding to particular patterns of light flashes

5   characteristic of their species. Some flash more often than others or during different hours, while other species give fewer but longer flashes. Many species produce light of a characteristic color: yellow, bluish-green, or reddish. Mating occurs when the female's display leads a male to her, and most females stop flashing after they mate. But in a few

10   species, a mated female will continue to flash, using a pattern that attracts males of other firefly species. A veritable *femme fatale*, she waits until an alien male gets close, then grabs and eats him. (Adapted from Campbell, Neil A., Lawrence G. Mitchell, and Jane B. Reece. *Biology*. 3rd ed. San Francisco: Benjamin Cummings, 2000)

16. This paragraph is organized by
    A. explaining the flashing patterns of fireflies.
    B. illustrating the cannablistic female firefly behavior.
    C. describing the process fireflies use to signal mates.
    D. giving examples of the length and color of fireflies' flashes.

PASSAGE #12
Read the passage below and answer the questions that follow.

1   Many overweight and obese individuals are trying to lose weight. Although it took several months and years to put on the extra weight, many of them are looking for a quick way to lose that weight. This attitude results in choosing quick-weight-loss diets that are not effective and may be harmful.

5   Some choose metabolic products, such as herbs or caffeine, to lose weight. Herbs have not been shown to speed the loss of fat, and caffeine shows little promise as a weight-loss aid.

     Others go on very-low-calorie diets, which severely restrict nutrients and can result in serious metabolic imbalances. Weight can be lost on this type of diet; much of the weight
10   lost will be lean protein tissue and/or water, not fat. This results in harm to the muscles (including the heart), loss of essential vitamins and minerals through the water loss, and dizziness and fatigue. Further, if one cuts calories, the metabolism slows; once this person goes off the diet, the metabolism remains slow and the body continues to use few calories—and the pounds come back.

15   Liquid protein diets operate on the theory that insulin is controlled and therefore more fat is burned. With this type of diet, ketosis will result. Ketosis will increase blood levels of uric acid, a risk factor for gout and kidney stones. There is not research evidence that carbohydrates lead to fat storage and weight; further, the excessive protein in this diet can damage the kidneys and cause osteoporosis.

20   Prescription drugs, such as Redux and Pondimin (fen-phen), curb hunger by increasing the level of serotonin in the brain. These were intended for the obese, but were banned in 1997 after the FDA found strong evidence that they could seriously damage the heart.

     Some people try crash diets to lose a moderate amount of weight in a very short period. These types of diets can damage several body systems, and have been proven not to work
25   because most of these individuals regain their weight. This yo-yo dieting causes many health problems and shortens lifespan. The best way to lose weight is to lose weight slowly (no more than one-half to one pound a week), eat properly and in moderation, and exercise. (Adapted from Anspaugh, David J., and Gene Ezell. *Teaching Today's Health.* 7th ed. San Francisco: Pearson, 2004)

17. For this passage, the author uses the overall organizational pattern that
    A. explains the effects of many quick-weight-loss diets.
    B. classifies the types of quick-weight-loss-diets.
    C. gives the effects of the prescription drugs Redux and Pondimin (fen-phen).
    D. contrasts liquid protein diets with very-low-calorie diets.

18. The third paragraph is organized by
    A. explaining how weight is lost on very low-calorie diets.
    B. describes the effects of very low-calorie diets.
    C. defines very low-calorie diets.
    D. argues against using a very low-calorie diet for weight loss.

PASSAGE #13
Read the passage below and answer the question that follows.

1   President Truman's decision to order the atomic bombings on the Japanese cities of
        Hiroshima and Nagasaki has been the subject of intense historical debate. Truman's
        defenders argue that the bombs ended the war quickly, avoiding the necessity of a costly
        invasion and the probable loss of tens of thousands of Americans' lives and hundreds of
5   Japanese lives. According to some intelligence estimates, an invasion might have cost
        268,000 American casualties, with Japanese costs several times that figure.

        Truman's defenders also argue that Hiroshima and Nagasaki were legitimate targets with
        both military bases and war industry, and their civilian populations had been showered
        with leaflets warning them to evacuate. Finally, they argue that two bombs were
10   ultimately necessary to end the war. They note that even after the atomic bomb had fallen
        on Hiroshima, the Japanese war minister implored the nation's Supreme Council "for one
        last great battle on Japanese soil—as demanded by the national honor. . . . Would it not
        be wondrous for this whole nation to be destroyed like a beautiful flower."

        Truman's critics argue that the war might have ended even without the atomic bombings.
15   They maintain that the Japanese economy would have been strangled by a continued
        naval blockade and forced to surrender by conventional firebombing. The revisionists
        also contend that the President had options apart from using the bombs. They believe that
        it might have been possible to induce a Japanese surrender by a demonstration of the
        atomic bomb's power or by providing a more specific warning of the damage it could
20   produce or by guaranteeing the emperor's position in postwar Japan.

        The revisionists also believe that estimates of potential American casualties were grossly
        inflated after the war to justify the bombing. Finally, they argue that the bomb might have
        been dropped mainly to justify its cost or to scare the Soviet Union. The Soviet Union
        entered the Japanese war August 8, and some revisionists charge that the bombings were
25   designed to end the war before the Red army could occupy northern China. (Adapted
        from Martin, James Kirby et al. *America and Its Peoples*. 5th ed. New York: Longman,
        2004)

19. For this passage, the author uses the overall organizational pattern that
   A. gives reasons that the bombing of Hiroshima and Nagasaki ended the war.
   B. argues for and against Truman's decision to bomb Hiroshima and Nagasaki.
   C. gives the sequence of events that led to the dropping of the bombs.
   D. explains causes for dropping atomic bombs on Hiroshima and Nagasaki.

PASSAGE #14
Read the passage below and answer the questions that follow.

1   Fungi have a number of practical uses for humans. Most of us have eaten mushrooms although we may not have realized that we were ingesting the fruiting bodies of subterranean fungi. In addition, mushrooms are not the only fungi we eat. The distinctive flavors of certain kinds of cheeses, including Roquefort and blue cheese, come from the
5   fungi used to ripen them. Highly prized gourmets are truffles, the fruiting bodies of certain mycorrhizal fungi associated with tree roots. The unicellular fungi, the yeasts, are important in food production. Yeasts are used in baking, brewing, and winemaking. Fungi are medically valuable as well. Some fungi produce antibiotics that are used to treat bacterial diseases. In fact, the first antibiotic discovered was penicillin, which is
10   made by the common mold called *Penicillium*. (Adapted fromCampbell, Neil A., Lawrence G. Mitchell, and Jane B. Reece. *Biology*. 3rd ed. San Francisco: Benjamin Cummings, 2000)

20. This paragraph is organized by
   A. describing how fungi ripens cheeses.
   B. defines fungi.
   C. classifies the types of fungi.
   D. gives examples of fungi uses for people.

2
Connections *Within* a Sentence

This item tests your ability to recognize an *explicit* or *implicit* relationship *within* a sentence. **Explicit** relationships are **obviously stated** using the relevant words from the following list to express the desired connection between ideas. **Implicit** relationships are only **suggested**, **hinted** at, or **implied** rather than clearly stated. Therefore, you must be able to recognize which words would best connect ideas within a sentence when the transition word is not provided.

You must be able to recognize the relationships among words, phrases, or clauses *within* a sentence. You will be given a passage to read; the question will take one sentence from the passage and ask you to identify the *relationship* between **parts** of that *one* sentence. When the relationship is not clearly stated but *implied*, an understanding of the writer's overall *pattern of organization* will help you identify the correct answer.

- Consider the following list of relationships. Remember to refer to the preceding section because it contains the *patterns of organizations*, which tie directly into the *relationships* of sentences.

• **Addition:**	Also, as well as, in addition, too, moreover, and, besides, furthermore, equally important, then, finally.
• **Cause/effect:**	If, therefore, thus, as a result, so.
• **Concession:**	Of course, certainly, granted.
• **Contrast:**	But yet, however, on the one hand/on the other hand, nevertheless, conversely, in contrast, still.
• **Comparison:**	Similarly, likewise, in the same way.
• **Example:**	For example, for instance, thus, as an illustration, namely, specifically.
• **Place/spatial order:**	Above, adjacent, at the side, in the back, in the front, in the foreground, in the background, in the distance, below, here, there.
• **Statement/clarification:**	Normally, namely, specifically, thus.
• **Summary:**	Hence, in short, in summary, in conclusion, finally.
• **Process/listing/time:**	First, second, third, next, then finally, afterwards, before, soon, later, meanwhile, subsequently, immediately, eventually, currently.

Exercises: Connections *Within a* Sentence

STUDY HINT:

Just as before, the following section of exercises pulls passages that you have already seen in one or more of the previous sections. Remember, the purpose of presenting you with the same passages in different sections is to imitate the state exit exam, which presents you with a passage and then asks you several different types of questions based on that one passage. Also, many of these skills are connected to each other.

For example, the author's purpose is closely connected to the pattern of organization and reinforced by tone, so it is important for you to see how one passage uses each of these skills for an overall effect. For example, the preceding section, Patterns of Organization, and this section, Relationships Within Sentences, and the next section, Relationships Between Sentences, are all so closely related that you will benefit from seeing how they tie into each other.

So, study smart. Compare these questions to each of the sections where the passages also appear, and think about the relationship between the skills.

PASSAGE #1
Read the following passage and answer the questions that follow.

1   Contrary to popular assumption, slavery was not usually based on racism, but on one of three other factors. The first was debt. In some cultures, an individual who could not pay a debt could be enslaved by the creditor. The second was crime. Instead of being killed, a murderer or thief might be enslaved by the family of the victim as compensation for their
5   loss. The third was war and conquest. When one group of people conquered another, they often enslaved some of the vanquished. Historian Gerda Lerner notes that the first people enslaved through warfare were women. When premodern men raided a village or camp, they killed the men, raped the women, and the brought the women back as slaves. The women were valued for sexual purposes, for reproduction, and for their labor. (Henslin, James M. *Sociology*. 6th ed. Boston: Allyn and Bacon, 2003)

1.   "When one group of people conquered another, they often enslaved some of the vanquished." (lines 5-6)
      The relationship of parts within the sentence above is
      A. contrast.
      B. cause and effect.
      C. process.
      D. summary.

2.   "The women were valued for sexual purposes, for reproduction, and for their labor." (lines 8-9)
      The relationship of parts within the sentence above is
      A. summary.
      B. addition.
      C. clarification.
      D. listing.

41

PASSAGE #2
Read the following passage and answer the question that follows.

1   Nonflowing bodies of water such as lakes become contaminated in stages. First, pollutants such as animal fertilizer, detergents, industrial waste, and sewage are dumped into the water supply. As a result, an accelerated growth of algae occurs. As algae growth skyrockets on a diet of inorganic pollutants, especially nitrogen and phosphorus, a

5   blanket of slime covers the water. Eventual death of the algae results in bacterial decomposition that consumes the oxygen present. This oxygen deficit kills fish and other lake inhabitants, many of which are valuable as food resources, and, as recently suggested, disrupts freshwater animals' endocrine systems. Eventually, the body of water becomes contaminated beyond use. (Adapted from Anspaugh, David J., and Gene Ezell. *Teaching Today's Health.* 7th ed. San Francisco: Benjamin Cummings, 2004)

3.   "As algae growth skyrockets on a diet of inorganic pollutants, especially nitrogen and phosphorus, a blanket of slime covers the water." (lines 3-5)
     The relationship of parts within the sentence above is
     A.   spatial order.
     B.   example.
     C.   addition.
     D.   cause and effect.

PASSAGE #3
Read the following passage and answer the question that follows.

1   Cyberliteracy is not purely a print literacy, nor is Internet literacy purely an oral literacy. Cyberliteracy is an electronic literacy—newly emerging in a new medium—that combines feature of both print and the spoken word, and the medium does so in ways that change how we read, speak, think, and interact with others. Once we see that online texts

5   are not exactly written or spoken, we begin to understand that cyberliteracy requires a special form of critical thinking. Communication in the online world is not quite like anything else. Written messages, such as letters (even when written on a computer), are usually created slowly and with reflection, allowing the writer to think and revise even as the document is chugging away at the printer. But electronic *discourse*—talking,

10   conversing, interacting—encourages us to reply quickly, often in a more oral style. In discourse, we blur the normally accepted distinctions, such as writing versus speaking, and conventions, such as punctuation and spelling. Normal rules about writing, editing, and revising a document do not make much sense in this environment. (Adapted from Shedletsky, Leonard J., and Joan E. Aitken. *Human Communication on the Internet.* Boston: Allyn and Bacon, 2004)

4. "Cyberliteracy is an electronic literacy—newly emerging in a new medium—that combines features of both print and the spoken word, and the medium does so in ways that change how we read, speak, think, and interact with others." (lines 2-4)
    The relationship of parts within the sentence above is
    A. definition.
    B. addition.
    C. cause and effect.
    D. summary.

PASSAGE #4
Read the following passage and answer the questions that follow.

1   Research shows that men communicate with women in the same way they do with other men. Men are not showing disrespect for their female conversational partners, but are simply communicating as they normally do. Women, too, communicate as they do not only with men but also with other women. (Adapted from DeVito, Joseph A. *Essentials of Human Communication.* 3rd ed. New York: Longman, 1999)

5. "Research shows that men communicate with women in the same way they do with other men." (lines 1-2)
    The relationship of parts within the sentence above is
    A.   example.
    B.   cause and effect.
    C.   comparison.
    D.   clarification.

PASSAGE #5
Read the following passage and answer the questions that follow.

5   Most women were assisted in childbirth not by a doctor but by a midwife. Most midwives were older women who relied on practical experience in delivering children. One midwife, Martha Ballard, who practiced in Augusta, Maine, delivered 996 babies with only 4 recorded fatalities. Skilled midwives were highly valued. Communities tried to attract experienced midwives by offering a salary or a rent-free house. In addition to
10 assisting in childbirth, midwives helped deliver the offspring of animals, attended the baptisms and burials of infants, and testified in court cases of illegitimate babies.

During labor, midwives administered no painkillers, except for alcohol. Pain in childbirth was considered God's punishment for Eve's sin of eating the forbidden fruit in the Garden of Eden. Women were merely advised to have patience, to pray, and during
15 labor, to restrain their groans and cries which upset the people near them.

After delivery, new mothers were often treated to a banquet. At one such event, visitors feasted on boiled pork, beef, poultry, roast beef, turkey pie, and tarts. Women from well-to-do families were then expected to spend three to four weeks in bed convalescing. Their attendants kept the fireplace burning and wrapped them in a heavy blanket in order to help them sweat out "poisons." Women from poorer families were generally back at work in one or two days. (Adapted from Martin, James Kirby, et al. *America and Its Peoples*. New York: Longman, 2004)

6. What is the relationship between parts of the following sentence?
    "In addition to assisting in childbirth, midwives helped deliver the offspring of animals, attended the baptisms and burials of infants, and testified in court cases of illegitimate babies." (lines 9-11)
    A. Addition
    B. Time
    C. Listing
    D. Summary

7. What is the relationship between parts of the following sentence?
    "After delivery, new mothers were often treated to a banquet." (line 16)
    A. Cause and effect
    B. Summary
    C. Addition
    D. Time

PASSAGE #6
Read the following passage and answer the question that follows.

1   Birds of a feather may kill together. Harris, the leader, would likely have enjoyed the respect and admiration from Klebold, who in turn would have felt uplifted by the praise he received from his revered buddy. In their relationship, the two boys got from one another what was otherwise missing from their lives—they felt special, they gained a
5   sense of belonging, they were united against the world. As Harris remarked, as he and his friend made last-minute preparations to commit mass murder: "This is just a two-man war against everything else." (Adapted from Fox, James Alan, and Jack Levin. *The Will to Kill*. Boston: Allyn and Bacon, 2001)

8. What is the relationship between parts of the following sentence?
    "In their relationship, the two boys got from one another what was otherwise missing from their lives—they felt special, they gained a sense of belonging, they were united against the world." (lines 3-5)
    A. Comparison
    B. Example
    C. Concession
    D. Time

PASSAGE #7
Read the following passage and answer the question that follows.

1   Each of the 2000 or so species of firefly has its own way to signal a mate. When a female sees flashes of light from a male of her species, she reacts with flashes of her own. If the male sees her flashes, he automatically gives another display and flies in the female's direction. Members of both sexes are responding to particular patterns of light flashes

5   characteristic of their species. Some flash more often than others or during different
     hours, while other species give fewer but longer flashes. Many species produce light of a
     characteristic color: yellow, bluish-green, or reddish. Mating occurs when the female's
     display leads a male to her, and most females stop flashing after they mate. But in a few
10   species, a mated female will continue to flash, using a pattern that attracts males of other
     firefly species. A veritable *femme fatale*, she waits until an alien male gets close, then
     grabs and eats him. (Adapted from Campbell, Neil A., Lawrence G. Mitchell, and Jane B.
     Reece. *Biology*. 3rd ed. San Francisco: Benjamin Cummings, 2000)

9.   What is the relationship between parts of the following sentence?
     "Some flash more often than others or during different hours, while other species give
     fewer but longer flashes." (lines 5-6)
     A. Comparison
     B. Addition
     C. Contrast
     D. Process

PASSAGE #8
Read the following passage and answer the question that follows.

1   The dramatic difference between the social status of the Egyptian nobility and that of the
     common people is reflected in their respective burial rites. The keen Egyptian interest in
     the afterlife, combined with strikingly materialistic criteria for happiness, made lavish
     tombs for the pharaohs (Egyptian rulers) seem particularly important. Elaborate goods
5   were buried with the pharaoh to assure him a gracious existence in the world beyond, and
     a processional causeway linked each pyramid to a temple constructed for the worship of
     the pharaoh; adjacent to the pyramid was a building to house the special cedar boat that
     would carry him on his voyage to the land of the dead. The pyramid served as the core of
     an entire necropolis, or city of the dead, which included small pyramids for the wives and
10   daughters of the pharaoh and mastabas for the nobility. Even a minor royal official spent
     a considerable portion of his time preparing an elaborate tomb for his afterlife, and he
     would want his corpse to be mummified because of the Egyptian belief that the *ka*, the
     spirit of life in each person, periodically returned to the body. The corpse of an average
     farmer, however, was typically wrapped in a piece of linen and deposited in a cave or pit
15   with only a staff and a pair of sandals to facilitate the journey to the next world; some
     bodies were even left in the open sand of the desert. (Adapted from Greaves, Richard L.,
     Robert Zaller, and Jennifer Tolbert Roberts. *Civilizations of the West*. 2nd ed. New York:
     Longman, 1997)

10. What is the relationship between parts of the following sentence?
     "Elaborate goods were buried with the pharaoh to assure him a gracious existence in the
     world beyond, and a processional causeway linked each pyramid to a temple constructed
     for the worship of the pharaoh; adjacent to the pyramid was a building to house the
     special cedar boat that would carry him on his voyage to the land of the dead." (lines 4-8)
     A. Listing
     B. Time
     C. Spatial order
     D. Addition

3
Connections *Between* Sentences

This section tests your ability to recognize **stated** or **implied** relationships between sentences. You must be able to identify how ideas are connected; determine the relationship between specific sentences. You will be given a passage to read; the question will take *two sentences* from the passage and ask you to identify the relationship *between* those *sentences*.

When the relationship is not clearly stated but implied, an understanding of the writer's overall pattern of organization will help you identify the correct answer. Consider the following list (provided in the two preceding sections and repeated here for your convenience) as you complete the following practice exercises.

Study Hint:

If the relevant transition word is implied, not provided by being explicitly stated, then insert between the given sentences the word(s) for the choices of relationships listed in the questions option. For example, if the option A gives "Cause and effect" as a possible answer, then insert a cause and effect word like "therefore," and then re-read the two sentences to see if the word makes sense. If not, go to the next option and insert a word related to its pattern of organization.

Just remember to try a variety of words from any one pattern, for each word expresses a definite relationship.

• **Addition:**	Also, as well as, in addition, too, moreover, and, besides, furthermore, equally important, then, finally.
• **Cause/effect:**	If, therefore, thus, as a result, so.
• **Concession:**	Of course, certainly, granted.
• **Contrast:**	But yet, however, on the one hand/on the other hand, nevertheless, conversely, in contrast, still.
• **Comparison:**	Similarly, likewise, in the same way.
• **Example:**	For example, for instance, thus, as an illustration, namely, specifically.
• **Place/spatial order:**	Above, adjacent, at the side, in the back, in the front, in the foreground, in the background, in the distance, below, here, there.
• **Statement/clarification:**	Normally, namely, specifically, thus.
• **Summary:**	Hence, in short, in summary, in conclusion, finally.
• **Process/ listing/ time:**	First, second, third, next, then finally, afterwards, before, soon, later, meanwhile, subsequently, immediately, eventually, currently.

Exercises: Connections *Between* Sentences

PASSAGE #1
Read the following passage and answer the questions that follow.

1   One factor that affects the formation of friendship in prisons is the duration of the
sentence. Three stages of short-term (one or two years) inmate adaptation are typical.
First, inmates experience uncertainty and fear, based on their images of what life is like
in prison. Therefore, they avoid contact with other prisoners and guards as much as
5   possible. The next stage involves the creation of a survival niche. The prisoner has
selective interactions with other inmates and may develop a "partnership" with another
inmate. Partners hang around together and watch out for each other. Maintaining a close
tie with another inmate is difficult. In the third phase, the prisoner anticipates his eventual
release, transfers to a minimum security area, increases contact with outside visitors, and
10   begins the transition to the outside. In this stage, partners begin to detach from each other
as one of the pair moves toward the outside world. (Adapted from Miller, Barbara D.
Cultural Anthropology. 2nd ed. Boston: Allyn and Bacon, 2002)

1.   The implied relationship between the third and fourth sentences (lines 3-5) of the above
paragraph is
A. summary.
B. comparison.
C. process.
D. cause and effect.

2.   The implied relationship between the sixth and seventh sentences (lines 5-7) of the above
paragraph is
A. comparison.
B. cause and effect.
C. addition.
D. restatement.

PASSAGE #2
Read the following passage and answer the question that follows.

1   As a result of Robert Fulton's construction of the North River Steamboat in 1907, the day
of the steamboat had dawned. In the 1820s its major effects were clear. The great
Mississippi Valley, in the full tide of its development, was immensely enriched. Produce
poured down to New Orleans, which soon ranked with New York and Liverpool among
5   the world's great ports. Only 80,000 tons of freight reached New Orleans from the
interior in 1816 and 1817. Later, in 1840 and 1841, more than 542,000 tons of freight
were transported. Upriver traffic was affected even more spectacularly. Freight charges
plummeted, in some cases to a tenth of what they had been after the War of 1812. Around
1818, coffee cost 16 cents a pound more in Cincinnati than in New Orleans, a decade
10   later less than 3 cents more. The Northwest emerged from self-sufficiency with a rush
and became part of the national market. (Adapted from Garraty, John A., and Mark C.
Carnes. *The American Nation*. 10th ed. New York: Longman, 2000)

47

3. The implied relationship between the fourth and fifth sentences (lines 5-7) of the above paragraph is
   A. contrast.
   B. example.
   C. time order.
   D. addition.

PASSAGE #3
Read the passage below and answer the questions that follow.

1   Different things motivate different people: A monk is not motivated to make money; an entrepreneur is not motivated to give away all earthly possessions and seek enlightenment on a mountaintop. Moreover, you are not motivated by the same forces day in and day out; rather, motivation comes to the fore when you have a *need* or a *want*. A **need** is a

5   condition that arises from the lack of a requirement. Needs give rise to drives, which push you to reach a particular goal that will reduce the need. For example, lacking nutrients creates a need; hunger is a drive that will lead you to fill that need. In contrast, a **want** is a condition that arises when you have an unmet goal that will not fill a requirement. A want causes the goal to act as an incentive. You might *need* to eat, but you don't *need* a

10   fancier car, although you might desperately *want* one—and the promise of a new car for working hard over the summer would be an incentive for you to put in long hours on the job. You are not necessarily aware of your needs or wants; **implicit motives** are needs and wants that direct your behavior unconsciously. (Adapted from Kosslyn, Stephen M., and Robin S. Rosenberg. *Psychology*. 2nd ed. Boston: Allyn and Bacon, 2004)

4. Identify the relationship between these two sentences from the above paragraph.
   "Different things motivate different people: A monk is not motivated to make money, an entrepreneur is not motivated to give away all earthly possessions and seek enlightenment on a mountaintop. Moreover, you are not motivated by the same forces day in and day out; rather, motivation comes to the fore when you have a *need* or *want*." (lines 1-4)
   The second sentence
   A. exemplifies (is an example of) the first.
   B. adds to the first.
   C. shows the effect of the first.
   D. contrasts the first.

5. Identify the relationship between these two sentences from the above paragraph.
   "Needs give rise to drives, which push you to reach a particular goal that will reduce the need. Lacking nutrients creates a need; hunger is a drive that will lead you to fill that need." (lines 5-7)
   The second sentence
   A. exemplifies (is an example of) the first.
   B. summarizes the first.
   C. defines the first.
   D. compares with the first.

PASSAGE #4
Read the passage below and answer the questions that follow.

1   North America has ten species of skunks. The one most people have seen—or at least smelled—is the abundant and widespread striped skunk. Another species is the spotted skunk, rarely seen but especially interesting because it illustrates some important concepts about biological species. This particular skunk belongs to a species called the
5   western spotted skunk. The adult is only about the size of a house cat, but it has a potent chemical arsenal that makes up for its small size. Before spraying her potent musk, a female guarding her young usually warns an intruder by raising her tail, stamping her forefeet, raking the ground with her claws, or even doing a handstand. When all else fails, she can spray her penetrating odor for three meters with considerable accuracy.

10   The western spotted skunk inhabits a variety of environments in the United States, from the Pacific coast to the western Great Plains. It is closely related to the eastern spotted skunk, which occurs throughout the southeastern and midwestern United States. The ranges of these two species overlap, and the two species look so much alike that even experts can have a difficult time telling them apart. Both are black with broken white
15   stripes and spots. Individuals of the western species are, on average, slightly smaller, and some have a white tip on the tail, but these and other minor differences in body form are not always present.

For many years, biologists debated whether all spotted skunks belong to one species. But in the 1960s, studies of sexual reproduction in these animals showed that they are indeed
20   two species. Reproduction in the eastern spotted skunk is a straightforward affair. Mating occurs in late winter, and young are born between April and July. In marked contrast, the western spotted skunk includes what is called delayed development in its reproductive cycle. Mating takes place in the later summer and early fall, and zygotes begin to develop in the uterus of the female. Further development, however, is temporarily stopped at an
25   early point called the blastocyst stage. Blastocysts remain dormant in the female's uterus throughout the winter months and resume growth in the spring, with the young (usually 5-7) being born in May or June. Because mating occurs at different times of the year for the two species, there is no opportunity for gene flow between populations of eastern and western spotted skunks. Thus, they are separate species, despite the pronounced
30   similarities in their body form and coloration.

Spotted skunks show us that looks can be deceiving. Without knowledge of the mating cycles, we could interpret the minor differences between the two species as insignificant and conclude that there is only one species of spotted skunk in North America. (Adapted from Campbell, Neil A., Lawrence G. Mitchell, and Jane B. Reece. *Biology*. 3rd ed. San Francisco: Benjamin Cummings, 2000)

6. Identify the relationship between these two sentences from the first paragraph.
    "Before spraying her potent musk, a female guarding her young usually warns an intruder by raising her tail, stamping her forefeet, raking the ground with her claws, or even doing a handstand. When all else fails, she can spray her penetrating odor for three meters with considerable accuracy." (lines 6-9)
    A. Contrast
    B. Cause and effect
    C. Example
    D. Addition

7. Identify the relationship between these two sentences from the second paragraph.
    "The ranges of these two species overlap, and the two species look so much alike that even experts can have a difficult time telling them apart. Both are black with broken white stripes and spots." (lines 4-6)
    A. Addition
    B. Example
    C. Summary
    D. Comparison

8. Identify the relationship between these two sentences from the third paragraph.
    "Further development, however, is temporarily stopped at an early point called the blastocyst stage. Blastocysts remain dormant in the female's uterus throughout the winter months and resume growth in the spring, with the young (usually 5-7) being born in May or June." (lines 24-27)
    The second sentence
    A. adds to the first.
    B. restates the first.
    C. defines the first.
    D. follows the first in time.

PASSAGE #5
Read the passage below and answer the questions that follow.

1   In the 1980s, a long-running TV public service advertisement showed a father confronting his son with what is obviously the boy's drug paraphernalia. The father asks his son incredulously, "Where did you learn to do this?" The son, half in tears, replies, "From you, okay? I learned it from watching you!" Observational learning, which results
5   simply from watching others, clearly appears to be a factor in an adolescent's willingness to experiment with drugs and alcohol.

    Andrews and her colleagues found that adolescents' relationships with their parents influence whether they will model the substance use patterns of the parents. Specifically, they found that adolescents who had a positive relationship with their mothers modeled
10 her use (or nonuse) of cigarettes, and those who had a close relationship with their fathers modeled the father's marijuana use (or nonuse). Similarly, those who had a negative relationship with their parents were less likely to model their parents' use of drugs or alcohol. Although some of the more complex results of this study depended on the age and sex of the adolescent, the general findings can be understood by thinking about them

50

15   from the three levels of analysis and their interactions.

At the level of the brain, observing someone engage in a behavior causes you to store new memories, which involves the hippocampus and related brain systems. These memories later can guide behavior, as they do in all types of imitation. At the level of the

20   person, if you are motivated to observe someone, you are likely to be paying more attention to him or her and, therefore, increasing the likelihood of your learning from them and remembering what you learn. At the level of the group, you are more likely to be captivated by models who have certain attractive characteristics.

In this case, adolescents who had a positive relationship with their parents were more likely to do what their parents did; if their parents didn't smoke, the adolescents were less

25   likely to do so. The events at these levels interact. Children who enjoy a positive relationship with their parents may agree with their parents' higher status than do children who have a negative relationship with their parents. Thus, the former group of children probably increases the amount of attention they give to their parents' behavior. (Adapted from Kosslyn, Stephen M., and Robin S. Rosenberg. *Psychology.* 2nd ed. Boston: Allyn and Bacon, 2004)

9.   Identify the relationship between these two sentences from the second paragraph.
"Andrews and her colleagues found that adolescents' relationships with their parents influence whether they will model the substance use patterns of the parents. Specifically, they found that adolescents who had a positive relationship with their mothers modeled her use (or nonuse) of cigarettes, and those who had a close relationship with their fathers modeled the father's marijuana use (or nonuse)."
The second sentence
A. adds to the first.
B. shows the effect of the first.
C. exemplifies (is an example of) the first.
D. clarifies the first.

10.   Identify the relationship between these two sentences from the third paragraph.
"The events at these levels interact. Children who enjoy a positive relationship with their parents may agree with their parents' higher status than do children who have a negative relationship with their parents." (lines 25-27)
A. Clarification
B. Contrast
C. Cause and effect
D. Summary

CHAPTER 3: *LANGUAGE SKILLS*

1
Word Choice: Context Clues

This section tests your ability to determine the meaning of a word or phrase *according to its context*. *Context* is known as the *language* that *surrounds* a word that helps to *determine* its *meaning*. Context gives clues to the meaning of unfamiliar words or terms. You will be given a passage to read from where words will be identified that you may not know. You must choose from several options the word or phrase that has the same meaning as the word from the passage. Apply the following *context clues* to choose your answer.

- **Definitions:** Immediately following the word, an author may provide a definition word set off by commas, parentheses, or dashes. The following definition clue words may also be used: is, refers to, can be defined, or, such as.

    Example: 1. The scientific revolution had reordered Western people's views of the <u>cosmos</u> *(the universe, which is considered in harmony and well-ordered)* and themselves.

    2. The <u>nobility</u>—*kings and their courts*—was still predominant.

    3. The British East India Company held a <u>monopoly</u>—*total control of the market*—of all trade between India and the rest of the Empire.

    4. The crowd <u>milled</u>, *confused and aimless*, in the streets.

- **Synonyms:** Often, an author provides another word of **similar** meaning. Synonyms use the same kinds of punctuation and clue words as definitions.

    Example: 1. The nobility was still <u>predominant</u> (powerful).

    2. For a generation all of Europe was caught up in the <u>convulsive</u>—*shuddering*—changes.

    3. A substantial British tax was <u>levied</u> (charged) on the tea as well as the threepenny Townshed duty (tax).

    4. Crowds milled in the streets, <u>harangued</u>—*scolded and criticized*—by Adams and his friends.

- **Examples:** Authors, also, include examples to illustrate or explain a word.

    Example: 1. America could hardly hold a national <u>referendum</u> *such as a direct public vote* on every policy issue on the government agenda.

    2. Members of Congress may spend so much of their time servicing their <u>constituencies</u> *such as the tobacco industry* that they have little time to be involved in the policy making process.

- **Antonyms:** Often, an author provides another word of **opposite** meaning to help you understand the full meaning through a contrast.

    Example: 1. Both political parties have long treated Social Security's benefits as <u>sacrosanct</u> rather than as *loot* to be used *disrespectfully, wastefully.*

52

2. Your essays reveal a good deal about your level of mastery of the course content as well as your ability to organize and <u>synthesize</u>; instead of *isolating* skills, you must apply them. Many times, you must rely on your ability to use the details of the entire passage to reason out the logical meaning of an unknown word.

- **General sense of the passage:**

Example: *If Parliament* could *grant* the East India Company a *monopoly* of the tea trade, it could *parcel (give)* out all or any part of American commerce to whomever *it pleased.* More important, the act appeared utterly <u>diabolical</u>, a <u>dastardly</u> *trick* to *trap* them into paying the tea tax. (notice how negative the information is throughout the passage, which hints at the ideas of diabolical (evil) and dastardly (mean and cowardly).

Study Hint:

Have you noticed how difficult many of the passages in this workbook are? That is because these passages have been taken from the very textbooks you just may use in your college classrooms, and the language is advanced. This is a very important skill for you to master.

As you read these passages, why not take the time to work with the words you don't know. Imitate the examples above and make up context clue cards for the words that get in the way of your understanding. Use your dictionary and thesaurus and write out definitions, synonyms, examples, antonyms. Or reword the sentences around the unfamiliar word using your own words to see if you can guess the meaning of the word that you don't know.

The key to understanding begins with words—one word at a time. Invest the time in your own success and develop a strong vocabulary!

Exercises: Word Choice: Context Clues

PASSAGE #1
Read the following passage and answer the questions that follow.

1   Future teachers not only need to consider the kind of students they will be working with; they also need to think seriously about the kind of work they will be doing. Some prospective teachers, not particularly fond of any academic subject, may gravitate toward elementary, early childhood, or special education, where they believe the emphasis will
5   be on "getting along with the kids." They think much of the school day will be filled with games and activities. The human side of teaching will be fun and rewarding. As for the academic side, surely they will know more than their students. Besides, a number of people—including some teachers and administrators—have told them you don't have to be very smart to be a teacher. They may even have heard that being too bright can hurt.

10   Let me dispel several myths about teaching. In spite of all the publicity about teacher burnout, some people cling to the belief teaching is a fun job. It is not. Getting through to students can certainly be rewarding, but reaching them takes hour after hour of effort. Fun is not the right word. Listen to the counsel of a Florida teacher: "Teaching is work. It is the hardest job there is. Learning is work. We try to make it enjoyable, interesting,
15   exciting, motivating, relevant, palatable, etc. But any way you slice it, it's work."

Notwithstanding the public outcry over academically incompetent teachers, some people believe another myth. Rudimentary literacy is the only academic qualification teachers of the youngest or least able students must have. It is not. This myth, another holdover from the past, finds no support in the research on teacher effectiveness. (Newman, Joseph W. *America's Teachers: An Introduction to Education.* 4th ed. Boston: Allyn and Bacon, 2002)

1.   As used in line 3, the word <u>gravitate</u> means
     A. be sympathetic.
     B. be attracted.
     C. be agreeable.
     D. be prejudiced.

2.   The word <u>dispel</u> (line 10) means
     A. describe.
     B. explain.
     C. remove.
     D. expose.

3.   As used in line 16, <u>incompetent</u> most nearly means
     A. weak.
     B. irresponsible.
     C. unproductive.
     D. inadequate.

PASSAGE #2
Read the passage below and answer the following questions.

1   Today television is the most prevalent means used by candidates to reach voters. Thomas Patterson stresses that "today's presidential campaign is essentially a mass media campaign. . . . It is not exaggeration to say that, for the majority of voters, the campaign has little reality apart from its media version."

5   The most important goal of any media campaign is simply to get attention. Media coverage is determined by two factors: (1) how candidates use their advertising budget, and (2) the "free" attention they get as newsmakers. The first, obviously, is relatively easy to control; the second is more difficult but not impossible. Almost every logistical decision in a campaign—where to eat breakfast, whom to include on the rostrum, when to

10   announce a major policy proposal—is calculated according to its intended media impact. About half the total budget for a presidential or senatorial campaign will be used for television advertising.

      Candidates attempt to manipulate their images through advertising and image building, but they have less control over the other aspect of the media news coverage. To be sure,

15   most campaigns have press aides who feed "canned" news releases to reporters. Still, the media largely determine for themselves what is happening in a campaign. Campaign coverage seems to be a constant interplay between hard news about what candidates say and do and the human interest angle, which most journalists think sells newspapers or interests television viewers. (Adapted from Edwards, George C., Martin P. Wattenberg, and Robert L. Lineberry. *Government in America.* 9th ed. New York: Longman, 2000)

4.   As used in line 1, <u>prevalent</u> most nearly means
     A. modern.
     B. common.
     C. ordinary.
     D. powerful.

5.   The word <u>manipulate</u> (line 13) most nearly means
     A. control.
     B. use.
     C. apply.
     D. plan.

6.   As used in line 17, <u>interplay</u> means
     A. competition.
     B. relationship.
     C. link.
     D. interaction.

PASSAGE #3
Read the passage below and answer the questions that follow.

1   Ignorance of African geography and environment has contributed greatly to the
prevailing misconceptions about African culture and history. Many Americans, for
instance, have thought of the continent as an immense "jungle." In reality, more than half
of the area south of the Sahara consists of grassy plains known as *savanna*, whereas
5   "jungle" or tropical rain forests takes up just seven percent of the land surface.

The most habitable areas have been the savannas, their grasslands and trees favoring both
human settlement and long-distance trade and agriculture. The northern savanna stretches
across the continent just south of the central desert, the Sahara. Other patches of savanna
are interspersed among the mountains and lakes of East Africa and another belt of
10   grassland that runs east and west across southern Africa, north and east of the Kalahari
Desert.

Between the northern and southern savannas, in the region of the equator, is dense rain
forest. Although the rain forest is lush, its soils are poor because torrential rains cause soil
erosion and intense heat leaches the soil of nutrients and burns off humus or organic
15   matter that is essential for soil fertility. The rain forests also harbor insects that carry
deadly diseases. Mosquitoes transmit malaria and yellow fever, and the tsetse fly is a
carrier of sleeping sickness to which both humans and animals, such as horses and cattle,
are susceptible. (Brummet, Palmira, et al. *Civilization*. 9th ed. New York: Longman,
2000)

7.   As used in line 6, <u>habitable</u> most nearly means
A. livable.
B. convenient.
C. spacious.
D. fertile.

8.   The word <u>interspersed</u> in line 9 most nearly means
A. located.
B. planted.
C. scattered.
D. hidden.

9.   As used in line 14, <u>humus</u> means
A. sewage.
B. organic matter.
C. nutrients.
D. chemicals.

10.   The word <u>erosion</u> (line 14) most nearly means
A. destruction.
B. pollution.
C. washing away.
D. contamination.

2
Biased Language

This item tests your ability to detect a *positive* or *negative* bias or *subjective* point of view concerning a topic. You must be able to recognize the author's use of positive and negative language to relay a *strong opinion*.

You will be given a passage to read and then given four statements concerning the author's bias for or against the topic. Based on the passage, you must determine if the author is biased in favor of or is biased against a particular idea. Sometimes, authors use emotional language or include only the details that fit their opinions or personal viewpoints. Other times, authors act as reporters relaying information in an objective, factual manner.

Consider the following as you make your selection:
- Does the writer provide mostly positive information?
- Does the writer provide mostly negative information?
- Does the writer provide mainly factual details?
- Does the writer provide opposing views?

Exercises: Biased Language

PASSAGE #1
Read the passage below and answer the following questions.

1   Many overweight and obese individuals are trying to lose weight. Although it took several months and years to put on the extra weight, many of them are looking for a quick way to lose that weight. This attitude results in choosing quick-weight-loss diets that are not effective and may be harmful.

5   Some choose metabolic products, such as herbs or caffeine, to lose weight. Herbs have not been shown to speed the loss of fat, and caffeine shows little promise as a weight-loss aid.

     Others go on very low-calorie diets, which severely restrict nutrients and can result in serious metabolic imbalances. Weight can be lost on this type of diet; much of the weight
10   lost will be lean protein tissue and/or water, not fat. This results in harm to the muscles (including the heart), loss of essential vitamins and minerals through the water loss, and dizziness and fatigue. Further, if one cuts calories, the metabolism slows; once this person goes off the diet, the metabolism remains slow and the body continues to use few calories—and the pounds come back.

15   Liquid-protein diets operate on the theory that insulin is controlled and therefore more fat is burned. With this type of diet, ketosis will result. Ketosis will increase blood levels of uric acid, a risk factor for gout and kidney stones. There is no research evidence that carbohydrates lead to fat storage and weight; further, the excessive protein in this diet can damage the kidneys and cause osteoporosis.

20   Prescription drugs, such as Redux and Pondimin (fen-phen), curb hunger by increasing the level of serotonin in the brain. These were intended for the obese, but were banned in 1997 after the FDA found strong evidence that they could seriously damage the heart.

      Some people try crash diets to lose a moderate amount of weight in a very short period. These types of diets can damage several body systems and have been proved not
25   to work because most of these individuals regain their weight. This yo-yo dieting causes many health problems and shortens lifespan. The best way to lose weight is to lose weight slowly (no more than one-half to one pound a week), eat properly and in moderation, and exercise. (Adapted from Anspaugh, David J., and Gene Ezell. *Teaching Today's Health*. 7th ed. San Francisco: Pearson, 2004)

1.   In this passage, the author expresses a bias in favor of
      A. taking prescription drugs to lose weight.
      B. controlling insulin levels to burn fat.
      C. restricting calories.
      D. losing weight slowly.

2.   In this passage, the author is biased against
      A. harmful quick weight-loss diets.
      B. moderating food choices.
      C. obesity.
      D. research evidence on quick weight-loss diets.

PASSAGE #2
Read the passage below and answer the following questions.

1   Television's portrayal of courts and trials is almost as dramatic as its portrayal of detectives and police officers—both often vary from reality. Highly publicized trials are dramatic, but rare. The murder trial of O. J. Simpson made headlines for months. Cable News Network even carried much of the pretrial and trial live. But in reality, most cases,
5   even ones in which the evidence is solid, do not go to trial.

      If you visit a typical American criminal courtroom, you will rarely see a trial complete with judge and jury. In American courts, 90 percent of all cases begin and end with a guilty plea. Most cases are settled through a process called **plea bargaining**. A plea bargain results from an actual bargain struck between a defendant's lawyer and a
10   prosecutor to the effect that a defendant will plead guilty to a lesser crime (or fewer crimes) in exchange for a state's not prosecuting that defendant for a more serious (or additional) crime.

      Critics of the plea-bargaining system believe that it permits many criminals to avoid the full punishment they deserve. The process, however, works to the advantage of both
15   sides; it saves the state the time and money that would otherwise be spent on a trial, and it permits defendants who think they might be convicted of a serious charge to plead guilty to a lesser one. (Edwards, George C., Martin P. Wattenberg, and Robert L. Lineberry. *Government in America*. 9th ed. New York: Longman, 2000)

3. In this passage, the author is biased against
   A. live television trial coverage.
   B. the guilty plea.
   C. O.J. Simpson's verdict.
   D. spending money on trials.

4. In this passage, the author expresses a bias in favor of
   A. television's portrayal of courts and trials.
   B. detective and police shows on television.
   C. plea bargaining.
   D. trial by jury for every criminal case.

PASSAGE #3
Read the passage below and answer the following question.

1   The most common stimulant is caffeine, which is contained in coffee, tea, cola drinks, and even chocolate. Caffeine is a mild stimulant that is often abused. Nonetheless, it is a drug and should be recognized as one that can lead to health problems.

5   Caffeine is absorbed rather quickly into the bloodstream and reaches a peak blood level in about thirty to sixty minutes. It increases mental alertness and provides a feeling of energy. However, high doses of caffeine can overstimulate and cause nervousness and increased heart rate. Caffeine can also cause sleeplessness, excitement, and irritability. In some cases, high doses of caffeine can induce convulsions.

10   Coffee or cola drinking, let alone chocolate eating, cannot be considered drug abuse by most commonly accepted standards. But some individuals seek out caffeine for its own sake in over-the-counter products and in illegal substances to produce a caffeine "high." Because it is not considered a dangerous drug, the opportunities for caffeine abuse are often overlooked. (Anspaugh, David J., and Gene Ezell. *Teaching Today's Health*. 7th ed. San Francisco: Benjamin Cummings, 2004)

5. In this passage, the author has a bias in favor of
   A. eating chocolate and drinking coffee and cola.
   B. considering caffeine a drug.
   C. using caffeine to produce a "high."
   D. using caffeine to increase mental alertness.

PASSAGE #4
Read the passage below and answer the following questions.

1   Through the Equal Employment Opportunity Commission, the federal government has classified some interview questions as unlawful. Some of the more important areas about which unlawful questions are frequently asked concern age, marital status, race, religion, nationality, physical condition, and arrest and criminal records. For example, it's legal to

5   ask applicants whether they meet the legal age requirements for the job and could provide proof of that, but it's unlawful to ask their exact age, even in indirect ways.

One strategy to deal with unlawful questions is to answer the part you do not object to and to omit any information you do not want to give. For example, if you're asked the unlawful question concerning what language is spoken at home, you may respond with a

10   statement such as "I have language facility in German and Italian" without specifying a direct answer to the question. Generally, this type of response is preferable to the one that immediately tells the interviewer he or she is asking an unlawful question. In many cases, the interviewer may not even be aware of the legality of various questions and may have no intention of trying to get at information you're not obliged to give.

15   On the other hand, recognize that in many employment interviews, the unwritten intention is to keep certain people out, whether it's people who are older or those of a particular nationality, religion, and so on. If you're confronted by questions that are unlawful and that you do not want to answer, and if the gentle method described above does not work and your interviewer persists, you might counter by saying that such

20   information is irrelevant to the interview and to the position you're seeking. Be courteous but firm. If the interviewer still persists, though it is doubtful that many would after these direct responses, you might note that these questions are unlawful and that you're not going to answer them. (Adapted from DeVito, Joseph A. *Essentials of Human Communication*. 3rd ed. New York: Longman, 1999)

6.   In this passage, the author is biased against

   A. answering unlawful questions.
   B. answering direct questions.
   C. answering closed questions.
   D. answering for proof of age.

7.   In this passage, the author has a bias in favor of
   A. immediately telling the interviewer that he or she is asking an unlawful question.
   B. answering an unlawful question.
   C. developing strategies to deal with unlawful questions.
   D. turning in the employer for asking unlawful questions.

PASSAGE #5
Read the passage below and answer the following question.

1   Hate sites began on the Internet in the mid-1990s, and their numbers expanded rapidly. Now hate groups in general across the nation are on the rise because of the Internet. Hate sites advocate violence toward immigrants, Jews, Arabs, gays, abortion providers, and others. Through the Internet, disturbed minds effectively fuel hatred, violence, sexism,

5   racism, and terrorism. Never before has there been such an intensive way for deprived people to gather to reinforce their prejudices and hatred. In one analysis of hate speech sites, the researchers found sophisticated use of persuasive strategies. The hate sites generally started with an objective approach that was straightforward and neutral in which they reinforced and strengthened the hate ideas that people already have. The

10   Internet provides a forum for people with prejudicial attitudes to speak out and act out. Hatemongers can create an online world where they reign supreme, a world of similar

minds, where they can gather with others to feel that their way is right and where they can design severe disruption for the on-ground world. (Adapted from Shedletsky, Leonard J., and Joan E. Aitken. *Human Communication on the Internet*. Boston: Allyn and Bacon, 2004)

8. In this passage, the author is biased against
   A. online commentaries.
   B. online messages among terrorists.
   C. immigrants.
   D. hate sites.

PASSAGE #6
Read the passage below and answer the following questions.

1 The thousands of McDonald's restaurants that dot the U.S. landscape—and increasingly the world—have a significance that goes far beyond the convenience of ready-made hamburgers and milk shakes. As sociologist George Ritzer says, our everyday lives are being "McDonaldized."

5 The Mcdonaldization of society, the standardization of everyday life, does not refer just to the robotlike assembly of food. Shopping malls offer one-stop shopping in controlled environments. Travel agencies offer "package" tours. They will transport middle-class Americans to ten European capitals in fourteen days. All visitors experience the same hotels, restaurants, and other scheduled sites, and no one need fear meeting a "real"

10 native. *USA Today* spews out McNews—short, bland, unanalytic pieces that can be digested between gulps of the McShake or the McBurger.

Efficiency brings dependability. You can expect your burger and fries to taste the same whether you buy them in Los Angeles or Beijing. Efficiency also lowers prices. But efficiency does come at a cost. Predictability washes away spontaneity, changing the

15 quality of our lives. It produces a sameness, a bland version of what used to be unique experiences. For good or bad, our lives are being McDonaldized, and the predictability of packaged settings seems to be our social destiny. (Adapted from Henslin, James M. *Sociology*. 6th ed. Boston: Allyn and Bacon, 2003)

9. In this passage, the author has a bias in favor of
   A. package travel tours.
   B. unique experiences.
   C. *USA Today* news reporting.
   D. consistency in food at McDonald's across the world.

10. In this passage, the author is biased against
   A. shopping at a mall.
   B. standardization of everyday life.
   C. McDonald's burgers.
   D. efficiency.

61

3
Tone of Passage

This item tests your ability to identify the tone (mood, feeling, or attitude) created by the author. You must be able to determine tone through the author's use of words, details and sentence structure. Tone words may include the following: excited, humorous, ironic, neutral, nostalgic, pessimistic, reverent, sarcastic, and serious. Remember that this skill is closely related to the author's purpose. The following chart presents possible relationships between purpose, tone, and type of language. Other combinations are possible. For this test item, you will be given a passage to read and then asked to choose a tone word that best describes the author's overall feeling or attitude within the passage.

EXAMPLES:

Purpose	Possible Tone	Possible Word Choice
To inform	instructional, neutral	objective, unbiased
To persuade	inspirational, convincing, shocking, insistent pessimistic	subjective, emotional
To entertain	humorous, excited, ironic	subjective, emotional
To describe	nostalgic, honest, clinical, graphic, reverent, neutral	subjective, emotional objective, unbiased

---

Exercises: Tone of Passage

PASSAGE #1
Read the following passage and answer the question that follows.

1   Efficiency brings dependability. You can expect your burger and fries to taste the same whether you buy them in Los Angeles or Beijing. Efficiency also lowers prices. But efficiency does come at a cost. Predictability washes away spontaneity, changing the quality of our lives. It produces a sameness, a bland version of what used to be unique
5   experiences. For good or bad, our lives are being McDonaldized, and the predictability of packaged settings seems to be our social destiny. (Adapted from Henslin, James M. *Sociology*. 6th ed. Boston: Allyn and Bacon, 2003)

1.   What is the overall tone of this passage?
    A. Humorous
    B. Pessimistic
    C. Critical
    D. Nostalgic

PASSAGE #2
Read the following passage and answer the question that follows.

1   Regardless of the type of job you have, you have to divide your time between work and school. The following suggestions will help you balance these two segments of your life. First of all, make sure that your supervisor knows you are attending college and that your job helps pay for it. He or she may be more understanding and helpful if he or she knows
5   you are a serious student. In addition, try to find a coworker who may be willing to switch work hours or take your hours if you need extra time to study. Next, if possible, try to build a work schedule around your class schedule. For example, if you have an eight-o'clock class on Tuesday mornings, try not to work until midnight on Monday night. Finally, allow study time for each class. Make sure you have time between class
10   sessions to do homework and complete assigned readings. For example, if you have a Tuesday/Thursday class, make sure you have some study time between the two sessions. (Adapted from McWhorter, Kathleen T. *Study and Critical Thinking Skills in College.* 5th ed. New York: Longman, 2003)

2.   The tone of this passage can best be described as
      A. instructive.
      B. authoritative.
      C. cautionary.
      D. sarcastic.

PASSAGE #3
Read the passage below and answer the question that follows.

1   Each of the 2000 or so species of firefly has its own way to signal a mate. When a female sees flashes of light from a male of her species, she reacts with flashes of her own. If the male sees her flashes, he automatically gives another display and flies in the female's direction. Members of both sexes are responding to particular patterns of light flashes
5   characteristic of their species. Some flash more often than others or during different hours, while other species give fewer but longer flashes. Many species produce light of a characteristic color: yellow, bluish-green, or reddish. Mating occurs when the female's display leads a male to her, and most females stop flashing after they mate. But in a few
10   species, a mated female will continue to flash, using a pattern that attracts males of other firefly species. A veritable *femme fatale*, she waits until an alien male gets close, then grabs and eats him. (Adapted from Campbell, Neil A., Lawrence G. Mitchell, and Jane B. Reece. *Biology.* 3rd ed. San Francisco: Benjamin Cummings, 2000)

3.   What is the overall tone of this passage?
      A. Humorous
      B. Objective
      C. Critical
      D. Argumentative

PASSAGE #4
Read the passage below and answer the question that follows.

1   Fungi have a number of practical uses for humans. Most of us have eaten mushrooms although we may not have realized that we were ingesting the fruiting bodies of subterranean fungi. In addition, mushrooms are not the only fungi we eat. The distinctive flavors of certain kinds of cheeses, including Roquefort and blue cheese come from the

5   fungi used to ripen them. Highly prized gourmets are truffles, the fruiting bodies of certain mycorrhizal fungi associated with tree roots. The unicellular fungi, the yeasts, are important in food production. Yeasts are used in baking, brewing, and winemaking. Fungi are medically valuable as well. Some fungi produce antibiotics that are used to treat bacterial diseases. In fact, the first antibiotic discovered was penicillin, which is

10   made by the common mold called *Penicillium*. (Adapted fromCampbell, Neil A., Lawrence G. Mitchell, and Jane B. Reece. *Biology*. 3rd ed. San Francisco: Benjamin Cummings, 2000)

4.   The tone of this passage can best be described as
     A. neutral.
     B. respectful.
     C. excited.
     D. boring.

PASSAGE #5
Read the passage below and answer the question that follows.

1   Plagiarism is a serious infraction in most settings. Students can be suspended or expelled from school. Researchers can lose their jobs and their standing in the academic community. Most importantly, plagiarism is serious because it violates several of the reasonable criteria for ethical decision making. Plagiarism violates your obligation to

5   yourself to be truthful, and it violates your obligation to society to produce fair and accurate information. It also violates your obligation to other students and researchers. (Adapted from Gurak, Laura J., and John M. Lannon. *A Concise Guide to Technical Communication*. New York: Longman, 2001)

5.   What is the overall tone of this passage?
     A. Cautionary
     B. Defiant
     C. Annoyed
     D. Sad

PASSAGE #6
Read the passage below and answer the question that follows.

1   Truman's critics argue that the war might have ended even without the atomic bombings. They maintain that the Japanese economy would have been strangled by a continued naval blockade and forced to surrender by conventional firebombing. The revisionists also contend that the President had options apart from using the bombs. They believe that

5   it might have been possible to induce a Japanese surrender by a demonstration of the
       atomic bomb's power or by providing a more specific warning of the damage it could
       produce or by guaranteeing the emperor's position in postwar Japan. (Adapted from
       Martin, James Kirby et al. *America and Its Peoples*. 5th ed. New York: Longman, 2004)

6.   The tone of this passage can best be described as
       A. complaining.
       B. passionate.
       C. neutral.
       D. humorous.

PASSAGE #7
Read the passage below and answer the question that follows.

1   On April 20, 1999, a school shooting of such immense proportions occurred which
       radically, if not permanently, altered public thinking and debate about student safety and
       security. After months of planning and preparation, 18-year-old Eric Harris and 17-year-
       old Dylan Klebold armed themselves with guns and explosives and headed off to
5   Columbine High School in Littleton, Colorado, to celebrate Adolph Hitler's birthday in a
       manner fitting their hero. By the time the assault ended with self-inflicted fatal gunshots,
       a dozen students and one teacher lay dead. (Adapted from Campbell, Neil A., Lawrence
       G. Mitchell, and Jane B. Reece. *Biology*. 3rd ed. San Francisco: Benjamin Cummings,
       2000)

7.   What is the overall tone of this passage?
       A. Sad
       B. Graphic
       C. Excited
       D. Flattering

PASSAGE #8
Read the passage below and answer the question that follows.

1   We, therefore, the Representatives of the United States of America, in General Congress,
       Assembled, appealing to the Supreme Judge of the word for the rectitude of our
       intentions, do, in the Name, and by the Authority of the good People of these Colonies,
       solemnly publish and declare, That these United Colonies are, and of Right ought to be
5   Free and Independent States; that they are Absolved from all Allegiance to the British
       Crown, and that all political connection between them and the State of Great Britain, is
       and ought to be totally dissolved; and that as Free and Independent States, they have full
       Power to levy War, conclude Peace, contract Alliances, establish Commerce, and to do
       all other Acts and Things which Independent States may of right do. And for the support
10   of this Declaration, with a firm reliance on the protection of divine Providence, we
       mutually pledge to each other our Lives, our Fortunes, and our sacred Honor. (from "The
       Declaration of Independence" in Edwards, George C., Martin P. Wattenberg, and Robert
       L. Lineberry. *Government in America*. 9th ed. New York: Longman, 2000)

8. The tone of this passage can best be described as
   A. reverent.
   B. nostalgic.
   C. objective.
   D. lofty.

PASSAGE #9
Read the passage below and answer the question that follows.

1   September 11, 2001
     Today, our fellow citizens, our way of life, our very freedom came under attack in a
     series of deliberate and deadly terrorist acts. The victims were in airplanes or in their
     offices: secretaries, business men and women, military and federal workers, moms and
5   dads, friends and neighbors. Thousands of lives were suddenly ended by evil, despicable
     acts of terror.

     The pictures of airplanes flying into buildings, fires burning, huge structures collapsing
     have filled us with disbelief, terrible sadness and a quiet, unyielding anger. These acts of
     mass murder were intended to frighten our nation into chaos and retreat. But they have
10   failed.

     Terrorist attacks can shake the foundations of our biggest buildings, but they cannot
     touch the foundation of America. These acts shatter steel but they cannot dent the steel of
     American resolve.

     Today, our nation saw evil, the very worst of human nature, and we responded with
15   the best of America, with the daring of our rescue workers, with the caring for strangers
     and neighbors who came to give blood and helped in any way they could. (Exerpts of
     President George W. Bush's speech on September 11, 2001 in Martin, James Kirby, et al.
     America and Its Peoples. 5ᵗʰ ed. New York: Longman, 2004)

9.   What is the overall tone of this passage?
     A. Impartial
     B. Passionate
     C. Inspirational
     D. Graphic

PASSAGE #10
Read the passage below and answer the question that follows.

1   It was a Tiwi custom when an old woman became too feeble to look after herself to
     "cover her up." This could only be done by her sons and brothers, and all of them had to
     agree beforehand so there would be no feud afterwards. My "mother" was now
     completely blind, she was constantly falling over logs or into fires, and they, her senior
5   clansmen, were in agreement that she would be better out of the way. The method was to
     dig a hole in the ground in some lonely place, put the old woman in the hole and fill it in
     with earth until only her head was showing. Everybody went away for a day or two and

then went back to the hole to discover to their surprise that the old woman was dead, having been too feeble to raise her arms from the earth. Nobody had "killed" her; her death in Tiwi eyes was a natural one. She had been alive when her relatives last saw her. I had never seen it done, though I knew it was the custom, so I asked my brothers if it was necessary for me to attend the "covering up." They said no and that they would do it, but only after they had my agreement. Of course I agreed, and a week or two later we heard in our camp that my "mother" was dead, and we walked and put on the trimmings of mourning. (Adapted from Henslin, James M. *Sociology*. 6th ed. Boston: Allyn and Bacon, 2003)

10.   The tone of this passage can best be described as
      A. graphic.
      B. annoyed.
      C. argumentative.
      D. excited.

CHAPTER 4: *REASONING SKILLS*

1
Fact and Opinion

This item tests your ability to distinguish between *fact* and *opinion*. You must be able to tell the difference between a statement that is *subjective*, or just a *personal belief*, and one that can be verified. You will be given a passage to read. A test question may pull a statement from the passage and ask you to identify the statement as a statement of fact or opinion. Another question may list as many as four sentences from the passage and ask you to choose the one that is a statement of fact, or in other questions, a statement of opinion.

- Remember, *facts* are statements that can be *verified* as *true* or *false*.

    EXAMPLE: Columbus died in 1506.

- *Opinions* express *attitudes, beliefs, feelings, personal experiences*, or *misleading statistics*.

    EXAMPLE: Conquistadores were brave and imaginative men well worthy of their fame.

Exercises: Fact and Opinion

PASSAGE #1
Read the passage below and answer the following question.

1   As a result of Robert Fulton's construction of the North River Steamboat in 1907, the day of the steamboat had dawned. In the 1820s its major effects were clear. The great Mississippi Valley, in the full tide of its development, was immensely enriched. Produce poured down to New Orleans, which soon ranked with New York and Liverpool among
5   the world's great ports. Only 80,000 tons of freight reached New Orleans from the interior in 1816 and 1817. Later, in 1840 and 1841, more than 542,000 tons of freight were transported. Upriver traffic was affected even more spectacularly. Freight charges plummeted, in some cases to a tenth of what they had been after the War of 1812. Around 1818, coffee cost 16 cents a pound more in Cincinnati than in New Orleans, a decade
10   later less than 3 cents more. The Northwest emerged from self-sufficiency with a rush and became part of the national market. (Adapted from Garraty, John A., and Mark C. Carnes. *The American Nation*. 10th ed. New York: Longman, 2000)

1.   Which sentence is a statement of opinion?
    A. Only 80,000 tons of freight reached New Orleans from the interior in 1816 and 1817.
    B. Later, in 1840 and 1841, more than 542,000 tons of freight were transported.
    C. Upriver traffic was affected even more spectacularly.
    D. Around 1818, coffee cost 16 cents a pound more in Cincinnati than in New Orleans, a decade later less than 3 cents more.

PASSAGE #2
Read the passage below and answer the following question.

1 The modern science of genetics began in the 1860s when an Augustinian monk named Gregor Mendel discovered the fundamental principles of genetics by breeding garden peas. Mendel lived and worked in an abbey in Brunn, Austria. In a paper published in 1866, Mendel correctly argued that parents pass on to their offspring discrete heritable
5 factors. He stressed that the heritable factors (today called genes) retain their individuality generation after generation. Mendel probably chose to study garden peas because they were easy to grow and available in many readily distinguishable varieties. Also, with pea plants, Mendel was able to exercise strict control over plant matings. As a result, he was always sure of the parentage of new plants. (Adapted from Campbell, Neil A., Lawrence G. Mitchell, and Jane B. Reece. *Biology*. 3rd ed. San Francisco: Benjamin Cummings, 2000)

2. Which sentence is a statement of opinion?
   A. The modern science of genetics began in the 1860s when an Augustinian monk named Gregor Mendel discovered the fundamental principles of genetics by breeding garden peas.
   B. Mendel lived and worked in an abbey in Brunn, Austria.
   C. Mendel probably chose to study garden peas because they were easy to grow and available in many readily distinguishable varieties.
   D. In a paper published in 1866, Mendel correctly argued that parents pass on to their offspring discrete heritable factors.

PASSAGE #3
Read the passage below and answer the following questions.

1 Ignorance of African geography and environment has contributed greatly to the prevailing misconceptions about African culture and history. Many Americans, for instance, have thought of the continent as an immense "jungle." In reality, more than half of the area south of the Sahara consists of grassy plains known as *savanna*, whereas
5 "jungle" or tropical rain forests take up just seven percent of the land surface.

The most habitable areas have been the savannas, their grasslands and trees favoring both human settlement and long-distance trade and agriculture. The northern savanna stretches across the continent just south of the central desert, the Sahara. Other patches of savanna are interspersed among the mountains and lakes of East Africa and another belt of
10 grassland that runs east and west across southern Africa, north and east of the Kalahari Desert.

Between the northern and southern savannas, in the region of the equator, is dense rain forest. Although the rain forest is lush, its soils are poor because torrential rains cause soil erosion and intense heat leaches the soil of nutrients and burns off humus or organic
15 matter that is essential for soil fertility. The rain forests also harbor insects that carry deadly diseases. Mosquitoes transmit malaria and yellow fever, and the tsetse fly is a

carrier of sleeping sickness to which both humans and animals such as horses and cattle are susceptible. (Brummet, Palmira, et al. *Civilization*. 9th ed. New York: Longman, 2000)

3. "Ignorance of African geography and environment has contributed greatly to the prevailing misconceptions about African culture and history." (lines 1-2)
   The above sentence is a statement of
   A. fact.
   B. opinion.

4. "Mosquitoes transmit malaria and yellow fever, and the tsetse fly is a carrier of sleeping sickness to which both humans and animals such as horses and cattle are susceptible." (lines 15-18)
   The above sentence is a statement of
   A. fact.
   B. opinion.

5. "Many Americans, for instance, have thought of the continent as an immense jungle.'" (lines 2-3)
   The above sentence is a statement of
   A. fact.
   B. opinion.

PASSAGE #4
Read the passage below and answer the following questions.

1   Though most precincts now use computer punch cards to record votes, the high-tech age has not yet made much impact on the voting process. There is good reason to expect that this will change in the twenty-first century.

      The National Mail Voter Registration Form is available to download on the Federal
5   Election Commission website. Twenty-two states currently accept copies of this application printed from the computer image, signed by the applicant, and mailed in the old-fashioned way. As e-mail becomes ever more popular and "snail mail" fades into a method reserved for packages, the entire voter registration process may someday be conducted mostly through electronic means. In an age where personal computers in the
10   home will be as common as television sets are today, this technology would clearly make registering to vote more user-friendly.

      If people can register by computer, the next step is naturally voting by e-mail. A growing trend in the Pacific Coast states has been voting by mail. In 1998, Oregon voters approved a referendum to eliminate traditional polling places and conduct all future
15   elections by mail. In California, 25 percent of the votes cast currently come in via the post office. Again, as e-mail takes the place of regular mail, why not have people cast their votes via cyberspace? It would be less costly for the state, as well as easier for the average citizen—assuming that computer literacy reaches near-universal proportions sometime in the future. The major concerns, of course, are currently being

20   addressed by some of the world's top computer programmers, as commercial enterprises look toward using the Internet to conduct business.

Making voting more user-friendly should encourage turnout, but people will still have to be interested enough in the elections of the future to send in their e-mail ballots. If everyone votes electronically in the convenience of his or her home, the sense of

25   community on election day may be lost, which could lead to lower turnout. (Adapted from Edwards, George C., Martin P. Wattenberg, and Robert L. Lineberry. *Government in America.* 9th ed. New York: Longman, 2000)

6.   "In California, 25 percent of the votes cast currently come in via the post office." (lines 15-16)
The above sentence is a statement of
A. fact.
B. opinion.

7.   "If everyone votes electronically in the convenience of his or her home, the sense of community on election day may be lost, which could lead to lower turnout." (lines 23-25)
The above sentence is a statement of
A. fact.
B. opinion.

8.   "If people can register by computer, the next step is naturally voting by e-mail." (line 12)
The above sentence is a statement of
A. fact.
B. opinion.

9.   The National Mail Voter Registration Form is available to download on the Federal Election Commission website. (lines 4-5)
The above sentence is a statement of
A. fact.
B. opinion.

PASSAGE #5
Read the passage below and answer the following question.

1   There is no military conscription at present. The United States has had a volunteer force since 1973. However, President Jimmy Carter asked Congress to require both men and women to register for the draft after the Soviet Union invaded Afghanistan in 1979. Registration was designed to facilitate any eventual conscription. In 1980, Congress

5   reinstated registration for men only, a policy that was not universally popular. Federal courts ordered registration suspended while several young men filed suit. These men argued that the registration requirement was gender-based discrimination that violated the due process clause of the Fifth Amendment.

The Supreme Court ruled in 1981 in *Rostker v. Goldberg* that male-only registration did

10   not violate the Fifth Amendment. The Court found that male-only registration bore a substantial relationship to Congress's goal of ensuring combat readiness and that Congress acted well within its constitutional authority to raise and regulate armies and

navies when it authorized the registration of men and not women. Congress, the Court said, was allowed to focus on the question of military need, rather than "equity." (Adapted from Edwards, George C., Martin P. Wattenberg, and Robert L. Lineberry. *Government in America.* 9th ed. New York: Longman, 2000)

10. Which sentence is a statement of opinion?
   A. The United States has had a volunteer force since 1973.
   B. In 1980, Congress reinstated registration for men only, a policy that was not universally popular.
   C. These men argued that the registration requirement was gender-based discrimination that violated the due process clause of the Fifth Amendment.
   D. The Supreme Court ruled in 1981 in *Rostker v. Goldberg* that male-only registration did not violate the Fifth Amendment.

2
Inferences and Conclusions

This section will test your ability to form *logical inferences* and *conclusions* about either an author's material or an *author's belief* based on the *context* of the passage. You will be given a passage to read. Then you will be presented with a series of statements, and you must choose the statement that expresses the most logical inference or conclusion that could be reached based on the *evidence in the passage*.

- Several skills discussed earlier will help you make the correct choice: author's purpose and tone. In addition to those skills, the following terms and definitions may be helpful.

  Denotation: the literal meaning of a word. For example, mother is a female who has given birth to an offspring.
  Connotation: the implied or suggested meaning of the word in addition to its literal meaning. For example, the word mother implies more than just a female who has given birth to an offspring; the word may imply love and security, or it may suggest stress and unhappiness depending on the individual's experience or information surrounding the word.
  Implication: an idea that is suggested or hinted at by the author but not directly stated. A man staggers, stumbles and slurs his words; the woman with him is distressed and trying to help him up. The implication is that the couple is experiencing some kind of trouble.
  Inference: a conclusion reached by the reader through reasoning based on known or assumed information. One observer of the man in the above example may infer that the man is drunk; another observer may conclude that the man is having a heart attack.

- When forming conclusions and drawing inferences, be sure that you understand the literal meaning of ideas, notice the writer's use of *connotations, details,* and *facts,* and *explain* the *reasons* for your thinking process.

Exercises: Inferences and Conclusions

PASSAGE #1
Read the passage below and answer the following questions.

1   During the seventeenth and eighteenth centuries, the process of childbirth in colonial America was conducted by women. The typical woman gave birth to her children at home, while female relatives and neighbors clustered at her bedside to offer support and encouragement.

5   Most women were assisted in childbirth not by a doctor but by a midwife. Most midwives were older women who relied on practical experience in delivering children. One midwife, Martha Ballard, who practiced in Augusta, Maine, delivered 996 babies with only 4 recorded fatalities. Skilled midwives were highly valued. Communities tried to attract experienced midwives by offering a salary or a rent-free house. In addition to
10   assisting in childbirth, midwives helped deliver the offspring of animals, attended the baptisms and burials of infants, and testified in court cases of illegitimate babies.

     During labor, midwives administered not painkillers, except for alcohol. Pain in childbirth was considered God's punishment for Eve's sin of eating the forbidden fruit in the Garden of Eden. Women were merely advised to have patience, to pray, and during
15   labor, to restrain their groans and cries which upset the people near them.

     After delivery, new mothers were often treated to a banquet. At one such event, visitors feasted on boiled pork, beef, poultry, roast beef, turkey pie, and tarts. Women from well-to-do families were then expected to spend three to four weeks in bed convalescing. Their attendants kept the fireplace burning and wrapped them in a heavy blanket in order to
20   help them sweat out "poisons." Women from poorer families were generally back at work in one or two days. (Adapted from Martin, James Kirby, et al. *America and Its Peoples*. New York: Longman, 2004)

1.   A conclusion that can be drawn from this passage is that during the seventeenth and eighteenth centuries,
     A. women from different social classes had different childbirth experiences.
     B. midwives received high salaries.
     C. doctors did not want to deliver babies.
     D. childbirth was conducted by women.

2.   What does the following sentence from the second paragraph suggest about midwives? "Skilled midwives were highly valued." (line 8)
     A. Skilled midwives were superior to doctors.
     B. Skilled midwives delivered babies without medicating the mothers.
     C. Skilled midwives were scarce.
     D. Midwives gave religious guidance to mothers.

Read the passage below and answer the following question.

1   In the 1980s, a long-running TV public service advertisement showed a father confronting his son with what is obviously the boy's drug paraphernalia. The father asks his son incredulously, "Where did you learn to do this?" The son, half in tears, replies, "From you, okay? I learned it from watching you!" Observational learning, which results
5   simply from watching others, clearly appears to be a factor in an adolescent's willingness to experiment with drugs and alcohol.

     Andrews and her colleagues found that adolescents' relationships with their parents influence whether they will model the substance use patterns of the parents. Specifically, they found that adolescents who had a positive relationship with their mothers modeled
10   her use (or nonuse) of cigarettes, and those who had a close relationship with their fathers modeled the father's marijuana use (or nonuse). Similarly, those who had a negative relationship with their parents were less likely to model their parents' use of drugs or alcohol. Although some of the more complex results of this study depended on the age and sex of the adolescent, the general findings can be understood by thinking about them
15   from the three levels of analysis and their interactions.

     At the level of the brain, observing someone engage in a behavior causes you to store new memories, which involves the hippocampus and related brain systems. These memories later can guide behavior, as they do in all types of imitation. At the level of the person, if you are motivated to observe someone, you are likely to be paying more
20   attention to him or her and, therefore, increasing the likelihood of your learning from them and remembering what you learn. At the level of the group, you are more likely to be captivated by models who have certain attractive characteristics.

     In this case, adolescents who had a positive relationship with their parents were more likely to do what their parents did; if their parents didn't smoke, the adolescents were less
25   likely to do so. The events at these levels interact. Children who enjoy a positive relationship with their parents may agree with their parents' higher status than do children who have a negative relationship with their parents. Thus, the former group of children probably increases the amount of attention they give to their parents' behavior. (Adapted from Kosslyn, Stephen M., and Robin S. Rosenberg. *Psychology.* 2nd ed. Boston: Allyn and Bacon, 2004)

3.   A conclusion that can be drawn from this passage is that
      A. adolescents model their parents' behavior.
      B. children with a positive relationship with their parents are more likely to use substances that their parents use.
      C. parents who drink set a poor example for their children.
      D. adolescents are willing to experiment with drugs and alcohol.

PASSAGE #3
Read the passage below and answer the following questions.

1   Deborah Tannen, sociologist and author, explains the differences in the listening behavior of men and women. Women seek to build rapport and establish a closer relationship and so use listening to achieve these ends. For example, women use more listening cues that let the other person know they are paying attention and are interested. On the other hand,
5   men not only use fewer listening cues but interrupt more and will often change the topic to one they know more about or one that is less relational or people-oriented to one that is more factual, for example, sports, statistics, economic developments, or political problems. Men, research shows, play up their expertise, emphasize it, and use it to dominate the conversation. Women play down their expertise.

10   Research shows that men communicate with women in the same way they do with other men. Men are not showing disrespect for their female conversational partners, but are simply communicating as they normally do. Women, too, communicate as they do not only with men but also with other women.

        Tannen argues that the goal of a man in conversation is to be accorded respect, and so he
15   seeks to display his knowledge and expertise even if he has to change the topic from one he knows little about to one he knows a great deal about. A woman, on the other hand, seeks to be liked, and so she expresses agreement and less frequently interrupts to take her turn as speaker.

        Men and women also show that they are listening in different ways. A woman is more apt
20   to give lots of listening cues, such as interjecting, "yeah, uh-uh," nodding in agreement, and smiling. A man is more likely to listen quietly, without giving lots of listening cues as feedback. Tannen also argues, however, that men do listen less to women than women listen to men. The reason is that listening places the person in an inferior position whereas speaking places the person in a superior position.

25   There is no evidence to show that these differences represent any negative motives on the part of men to prove themselves superior or of women to ingratiate themselves. Rather, these differences in listening are largely the result of the way in which men and women have been socialized. (Adapted from DeVito, Joseph A. *Essentials of Human Communication*. 3rd ed. New York: Longman, 1999)

4.   A conclusion that can be drawn from this passage is that
       A. men interrupt conversations more than women do.
       B. men and women do not communicate well.
       C. because men and women are socialized differently, their listening styles are different.
       D. a man's goal in conversation is to gain respect.

5. What does the following suggest about the way men listen?
"Tannen also argues, however, that men do listen less to women than women listen to men." (lines 22-23)
A. Men think women don't have anything interesting to say.
B. Men feel that listening puts them in an inferior position.
C. Men disrespect women.
D. Men seek to be liked, so they don't interrupt much.

PASSAGE #4
Read the passage below and answer the following questions.

1   On April 20, 1999, a school shooting of such immense proportions occurred which radically, if not permanently, altered public thinking and debate about student safety and security. After months of planning and preparation, 18-year-old Eric Harris and 17-year-old Dylan Klebold armed themselves with guns and explosives and headed off to
5   Columbine High School in Littleton, Colorado, to celebrate Adolph Hitler's birthday in a manner fitting their hero. By the time the assault ended with self-inflicted fatal gunshots, a dozen students and one teacher lay dead.

In understanding the horrific actions of schoolyard snipers, it is as important to examine friendships as it is to delve into family background. At Columbine, Harris and Klebold
10   were generally seen as geeks or nerds, from the point of view of any of the large student cliques—the jocks, the punks, etc. Though excluded from mainstream student culture, they banded together and bonded together with several of their fellow outcasts in what they came to call the "Trench Coat Mafia." The image they attempted to create was clearly one of power and dominance—the barbaric incivility, the forces of darkness, the
15   preoccupation with Hitler, the celebration of evil and villainy. Harris and Klebold desperately wanted to feel important; and in the preparations they made to murder their classmates, the two shooters got their wish. For more than a year, they plotted and planned, colluded and conspired to put one over on their schoolmates, teachers, and parents. They amassed an arsenal of weapons, strategized about logistics, and made final
20   preparations—yet, until it was too late, not a single adult got wind of what Harris and Klebold intended to do.

Birds of a feather may kill together. Harris, the leader, would likely have enjoyed the respect and admiration from Klebold, who in turn would have felt uplifted by the praise he received from his revered buddy. In their relationship, the two boys got from one
25   another what was otherwise missing from their lives—they felt special, they gained a sense of belonging, they were united against the world. As Harris remarked, as he and his friend made last-minute preparations to commit mass murder: "This is just a two-man war against everything else." (Adapted from Fox, James Alan, and Jack Levin. *The Will to Kill*. Boston: Allyn and Bacon, 2001)

6.   A conclusion that can be drawn from this passage is that
      A. it is important to understand family background and friendships of students who
         commit school shootings.
      B. students who are outcasts are likely commit acts of violence.
      C. schools are not safe.
      D. young people who are preoccupied with Hitler are mentally unstable.

7.   What does the following sentence from the third paragraph suggest about Harris and
      Klebold's motivation to commit mass murder?
      "This is just a two-man war against everything else." (lines 28-29)
      A. They wanted to imitate Hitler.
      B. They wanted to show that they were important.
      C. They wanted to get back at their parents.
      D. They thought their lives were not worth living.

PASSAGE #5
Read the passage below and answer the following question.

1   Few people work constantly at their jobs. Most of us take breaks and, at least once in a
      while, goof off. We meet fellow workers at the water cooler, and we talk in the hallway.
      Much of this interaction is good for the company, for it bonds us to fellow workers and
      ties us to our jobs.

5   Our personal lives may even cross over into our workday. Some of us make personal
      calls from the office. Bosses know that we need to check in with our child's preschool or
      make arrangements for a babysitter. They expect such calls. Some even wink as we make
      a date or nod as we arrange to have our car worked on. And most bosses make personal
      calls of their own from time to time. It's the abuse that bothers bosses, and it's not
10   surprising that they fire anyone who talks on the phone all day for personal reasons.

      The latest wrinkle at work is *cyberslacking*, using computers at work for personal
      purposes. Most workers fritter away some of their workday online. They trade stocks,
      download music, gamble, and play games. They read books, shop, exchange jokes, send
      personal e-mail, and visit online red-light districts. Some cyberslackers even operate their
15   own businesses online. Others spend most of their "working" hours battling virtual
      enemies. One computer programmer became a national champion playing *Starcraft* at
      work.

      Companies have struck back. Xerox fired 40 employees for downloading pornography at
      work. Dow Chemical fired 200 "workers" for cyberloafing. Then there is the cybersleuth.
20   With specialized software, cybersleuths can examine everything employees read online,
      everything they write, and every web site they visit. They can even bring up every word
      they've erased. What some workers don't know (and what some of us forget) is that
      "delete" does not mean *delete*. Our computer keeps a hidden diary, even of what we've
      erased. With a few clicks, the cybersleuth, like magic ink, makes our "deleted"

25   information visible, exposing our hidden diary for anyone to read. (Adapted from Henslin, James M. *Sociology*. 6th ed. Boston: Allyn and Bacon, 2003)

8.   A conclusion that can be drawn from this passage is that
      A. some employees operate their own online businesses at work.
      B. employers accept the fact that employees make personal phone calls at work.
      C. many employers have struck back at cyberslackers.
      D. viewing pornography online is addicting.

PASSAGE #6
Read the passage below and answer the following questions.

1   The analysis of DNA from fossils provides an opportunity to better understand extinct life and to trace the ancestry of genes found in modern organisms, including humans. Scientists have reported finding fragments of ancient DNA from many fossils, including a 40-million-year-old insect preserved in amber (fossilized plant resin), a 65-million-year

5   old dinosaur fossil, and a 30,000-year-old fossil arm bone of an extinct member of the human family tree (one of a group found in northern Europe called the Neanderthals).

In early autumn of 1991, two hikers working their way along the edge of a melting glacier in the high Alps of northern Italy found what seemed to be the weathered remains of an unlucky mountain climber. It was a man clothed in hand-sewn leather, frozen in

10   glacial ice. Next to him were a bow and several arrows, a wooden backpack, and a metal ax. A closer look turned up a leather pouch and other tools. The "Ice Man" turned out to be a leftover from the Stone Age, a young hunter who may have died from exhaustion and exposure some 5000 years ago.

Although scientists knew that the Ice Man was ancient, they did not know where he was

15   from. In 1994, researchers reported that mitochondrial DNA from the Ice Man closely matched that of central and northern Europeans, not Native Americans. Currently, the Ice Man remains frozen in the anatomy department of the University of Innsbruck. Continuing analysis of his DNA may provide more clues about his place in human evolution.

20   Science advances by the ebb and flow of ideas. Hypotheses are proposed, predictions made, and test results evaluated. Too often, however, the advance is highlighted by the popular press as though it involves only a forward march, and the importance of disproving a hypotheses is lost. Some of the research on fossilized DNA illustrates this key aspect of science. Because it is difficult to obtain uncontaminated samples from

25   fossils, ancient DNA is very challenging. Every report of success in isolating ancient DNA has been met with skepticism and further analyses to make sure the DNA traces were not contaminated with DNA from bacteria, fungi, or other organisms. DNA is unlikely to remain intact, except when organisms fossilize in extremely cold or dry places where organic material tends to be preserved. Contamination is a potential pitfall even in

30   ideal conditions. (Adapted from Campbell, Neil A., Lawrence G. Mitchell, and Jane B. Reece. *Biology*. 3rd ed. San Francisco: Benjamin Cummings, 2000)

9. What does the following sentence from the fourth paragraph suggest about science?
"Science advances by the ebb and flow of ideas." (line 20)
   A. The "Ice Man" discovered in 1991 was from the Stone Age.
   B. DNA is used as evidence to identify the perpetrator of a crime.
   C. Scientists have found ancient DNA in a 65-million-year-old dinosaur fossil.
   D. Advances in science are a result of a process including proposing hypotheses, making predictions, and evaluating results.

10. A conclusion that can be drawn from this passage is that
   A. ancient DNA analysis is challenging due to possible contamination.
   B. the Ice Man is one of the oldest humans ever discovered.
   C. the popular press does not always tell the whole story about a discovery.
   D. ancient insects have been preserved in amber.

PASSAGE #7
Read the passage below and answer the following question.

1   Today television is the most prevalent means used by candidates to reach voters. Thomas Patterson stresses that "today's presidential campaign is essentially a mass media campaign. . . . It is not exaggeration to say that, for the majority of voters, the campaign has little reality apart from its media version."

5   The most important goal of any media campaign is simply to get attention. Media coverage is determined by two factors: (1) how candidates use their advertising budget, and (2) the "free" attention they get as newsmakers. The first, obviously, is relatively easy to control; the second is more difficult but not impossible. Almost every logistical decision in a campaign—where to eat breakfast, whom to include on the rostrum, when to
10   announce a major policy proposal—is calculated according to its intended media impact. About half the total budget for a presidential or senatorial campaign will be used for television advertising.

    Candidates attempt to manipulate their images through advertising and image building, but they have less control over the other aspect of the media, news coverage. To be sure,
15   most campaigns have press aides who feed "canned" news releases to reporters. Still, the media largely determine for themselves what is happening in a campaign. Campaign coverage seems to be a constant interplay between hard news about what candidates say and do and the human interest angle, which most journalists think sells newspapers or interests television viewers. (Adapted from Edwards, George C., Martin P. Wattenberg, and Robert L. Lineberry. *Government in America*. 9th ed. New York: Longman, 2000)

11. A conclusion that can be drawn from this passage is that
   A. candidates spend the majority of their funds on television advertisements.
   B. news reporters determine what happens in a campaign.
   C. the press looks for opportunities to discredit presidential candidates.
   D. presidential candidates often criticize each other in their television advertisements.

12. What does the following sentence suggest about political campaigns?
" . . . It is not exaggeration to say that, for the majority of voters, the campaign has little reality apart from its media version." (lines 3-4)
   A. Campaigns are like television shows.
   B. Voters believe everything they see on television and read in the newspapers.
   C. Voters use the media as their primary source of information about candidates.
   D. The media creates the campaign that the public sees and hears.

PASSAGE #8
Read the passage below and answer the following questions.

1   The most common stimulant is caffeine, which is contained in coffee, tea, cola drinks, and even chocolate. Caffeine is a mild stimulant that is often abused. Nonetheless, it is a drug and should be recognized as one that can lead to health problems.

Caffeine is absorbed rather quickly into the bloodstream and reaches a peak blood level
5   in about thirty to sixty minutes. It increases mental alertness and provides a feeling of energy. However, high doses of caffeine can overstimulate and cause nervousness and increased heart rate. Caffeine can also cause sleeplessness, excitement, and irritability. In some cases, high doses of caffeine can induce convulsions.

Coffee or cola drinking, let alone chocolate eating, cannot be considered drug abuse by
10   most commonly accepted standards. But some individuals seek out caffeine for its own sake in over-the-counter products and in illegal substances to produce a caffeine "high." Because it is not considered a dangerous drug, the opportunities for caffeine abuse are often overlooked. (Anspaugh, David J., and Gene Ezell. *Teaching Today's Health.* 7ᵗʰ ed. San Francisco: Benjamin Cummings, 2004)

13. A conclusion that can be drawn from this passage is that
   A. the caffeine in coffee helps people stay awake by increasing mental alertness.
   B. people can get addicted to the caffeine in chocolate.
   C. caffeine is a drug that can lead to health problems.
   D. some people get so agitated from caffeine that they can't sleep.

PASSAGE #9
Read the passage below and answer the following question.

1   Hate sites began on the Internet in the mid-1990s, and their numbers expanded rapidly. Now hate groups in general across the nation are on the rise because of the Internet. Hate sites advocate violence toward immigrants, Jews, Arabs, gays, abortion providers, and others. Through the Internet, disturbed minds effectively fuel hatred, violence, sexism,
5   racism, and terrorism. Never before has there been such an intensive way for deprived people to gather to reinforce their prejudices and hatred. In one analysis of hate speech sites, the researchers found sophisticated use of persuasive strategies. The hate sites generally started with an objective approach that was straightforward and neutral in which they reinforced and strengthened the hate ideas that people already have. The

10   Internet provides a forum for people with prejudicial attitudes to speak out and act out. Hatemongers can create an online world where they reign supreme, a world of similar minds, where they can gather with others to feel that their way is right and where they can design severe disruption for the on-ground world. (Adapted from Shedletsky, Leonard J., and Joan E. Aitken. *Human Communication on the Internet*. Boston: Allyn and Bacon, 2004)

14.   A conclusion that can be drawn from this passage is that
    A. hate sites on the Internet give people with prejudices an opportunity to speak and act out and gain supporters.
    B. Internet hate sites are developed by people with personality disorders.
    C. hate sites encourage people to spread kill Jews, Arabs, gays, and abortion providers.
    D. terrorists use the Internet to encourage suicide bombings.

PASSAGE #10
Read the passage below and answer the following questions.

1   Evaluation research on drug education prevention programs done over the last thirty years indicates that these programs have not been effective. In fact, the findings state that these programs essentially had no effect on the drug problem. Although studies of the more recently developed programs are more optimistic, the findings still do not provide
5   strong evidence of highly effective programs.

       The goals of these programs have been to affect three basic areas: knowledge, attitudes, and behavior. The programs have had some success in increasing knowledge and, to a lesser extent, attitudes towards drugs; however, increases in knowledge and changed attitudes do not mean much if the actual drug behavior is not affected. In fact, those
10   programs that only increase knowledge tend to reduce anxiety and fear of drugs and may actually increase the likelihood of drug use. For example, one approach in the past was to provide students with complete information about all the possibilities of drug abuse, from the names of every street drug, to how the drugs are usually ingested, to detailed descriptions of possible effects of drugs and possible consequences of an overdose. Given
15   the inquiring nature of children, such an approach could well amount to a primer on how to take drugs, not how to avoid them.

       The only effective approach to drug education is one in which children come to see that drug abuse constitutes unnecessary and self-abusive consequences. Too often, the real appeal of such drugs as marijuana or alcohol is dismissed by asking children to take up a
20   sport or go bike riding or learn to play a musical instrument. Such suggestions are fine as far as they go, but they often fail to take into account the personal problems that may tempt children into drug abuse.

       Education programs that address social influence show that most promise in reducing or delaying onset of drug use. Psychological approaches in which social influences and
25   skills are stressed are more effective than other approaches. The most effective programs in influencing both attitudes and behavior are peer programs that included either refusal skills—with more direct emphasis on behavior—or social and life skills, or both.

81

The use of scare tactics in any health education program, including drug abuse education programs, is counterproductive. Children soon learn to recognize the difference between
30   fact and possible fiction. Attempts to equate the dangers of marijuana with those of heroin, suggestions that any drug can kill or permanently impair an individual, and other dire warnings, no matter how true, are often disregarded as propaganda. (Anspaugh, David J., and Gene Ezell. *Teaching Today's Health.* 7th ed. San Francisco: Benjamin Cummings, 2004)

15.   A conclusion that can be drawn from this passage is that
       A. Telling children to take up a sport instead of drugs is an effective tactic.
       B. Peer programs that teach social and life skills are the most effective in drug use prevention.
       C. The best approach for drug education is to avoid approaching it at all.
       D. Programs that increase knowledge about drugs are very successful.

16.   What does the following sentence from the passage suggest about scare tactics?
       "The use of scare tactics in any health education program, including drug abuse education programs, is counterproductive." (lines 28-29)
       A. Frightening children can cause psychological problems.
       B. Scare tactics may make drugs appealing.
       C. Children know more about drugs than their teachers do.
       D. Scare tactics work against the purpose of health education programs.

PASSAGE #11
Read the passage below and answer the following questions.

1   Matt Drudge was 30 years old when he broke his first story about Monica Lewinsky's relationship with President Clinton, which would become the biggest political scandal of the 1990s. Drudge had never been trained in journalism nor hired by any media outlet. He had neither verified the story nor done any extensive research on it. All he had to go on
5   was the rumor that *Newsweek* had been working on this story and had decided not to print it in that week's issue. But for Drudge, a rumor was good enough to report on. No editor was going to tell him that he needed confirmation, as Drudge worked on his own. He didn't have to worry about the damage to his publication because he didn't have one; he relied instead on getting the "Drudge Report" out through an e-mail list and by posting it
10   on his web site. When Drudge hit the enter button on his computer to post the Lewinsky story, he knew his life would be changed forever, and for quite some time so would the nation's.

       Matt Drudge and his brand of cyber reporting have changed the whole news cycle in America. Journalists who are working on a scoop know the can quickly lose an exclusive
15   story if someone like Drudge gets wind of it and posts the headline on the Internet. As a result, a number of newspapers immediately post their most important stories on their web site rather than waiting until the next morning. The *Dallas Morning News* made big headlines when they rushed a story onto the web about a White House steward testifying that he had seen President Clinton and Monica Lewinsky in a compromising position.
20   The next day the paper had egg on its face, however, when the steward's lawyer strongly denied the story and the paper was forced to retract it. Similarly, Drudge found himself in

trouble when he accused White House aide Sidney Blumenthal of spouse abuse. He quickly pulled the story and apologized when he realized it was planted by politically motivated Republican operatives, but not before Blumenthal hit him with a $30 million

25   libel suit.

Opinions on Matt Drudge and his reporting techniques vary widely. Because of his penchant for reporting rumors and gossip, the *New York Times* called him "the nation's chief mischief maker." Others have dubbed him the first Internet superstar and praised how he has paved the way for communication power to be transferred from media giants

30   to anyone with a modem. However one views him, it is clear that Matt Drudge has made a difference. (Adapted from Edwards, George C., Martin P. Wattenberg, and Robert L. Lineberry. *Government in America*. 9th ed. New York: Longman, 2000)

17.   A conclusion that can be drawn from this passage is that
       A. Matt Drudge made the Internet a player in news reporting.
       B. Matt Drudge's web site is one of the most popular news sites on the Internet.
       C. anyone can report the news on his or her own web site on the Internet.
       D. Matt Drudge likes to be the first to break a story.

18.   A conclusion that can be drawn from the first paragraph of this passage is that
       A. Matt Drudge is a troublemaker.
       B. Drudge's breaking of the Lewinsky story changed his life.
       C. Drudge enjoyed gathering and spreading rumors.
       D. Drudge broke the story about Monica Lewinsky's relationship with President Clinton.

PASSAGE #12
Read the passage below and answer the following questions.

1   Forest decline is not a new phenomenon. During the past two centuries, our forests have experienced several declines, with different species affected. What sets the current decline apart from all others is differences among the symptoms in the past and the similarity of symptoms among species today. Past declines could be attributed to natural

5   stresses, such as drought and disease. What causes forest decline and dieback today is not established, but the widespread similarity of symptoms suggests a common cause—air pollution. All of the affected forests are in the path of pollutants from industrial and urban sources.

      Forests close to the point of origin of pollutants experience the most direct effects of air

10   pollution, and their decline and death can be directly attributed to it. Little evidence exists that acid precipitation alone is the cause of forest decline and death at distant points. The effects of acid deposition, however, can so weaken trees that they succumb to other stresses such as drought and insect attack. The stressed forests of Fraser fir in the Great Smoky Mountains succumb to the attacks of the introduced balsam woolly adelgid. The

15   once deep, fragrant stands of Fraser fir, especially on the windward side and peaks of the Great Smoky Mountains, are now stands of skeleton trees.

Air pollution and acid rain also are altering succession by changing the species composition of forests. Just as the chestnut blight shifted dominance in the central hardwood forest from chestnut to oaks, so is air pollution shifting dominance from pines and other conifers to leaf-shedding trees more tolerant of air pollution. (Adapted from Smith, Robert Leo, and Thomas M. Smith. *Elements of Ecology*. 5th ed. San Francisco: Benjamin Cummings, 2003)

20

19. A conclusion that can be drawn from this passage is that
    A. forest dieback is due to drought and disease.
    B. pine trees are one of the few types of trees that are resistant to the effects of air pollution.
    C. air pollution and acid rain have caused decline and death of forests that are near industrial and urban areas.
    D. acid rain can weaken trees so that they become vulnerable to drought and insect attack.

20. What does the following sentence suggest about air pollution and acid rain?
    "Air pollution and acid rain also are altering succession by changing the species composition of forests." (lines 17-18)
    A. the types of trees growing in forests have changed because of air pollution and acid rain.
    B. air pollution and acid rain will eventually destroy all of our forests.
    C. the trees that are killed by air pollution and acid rain will become extinct.
    D. eventually, all species of trees will die from air pollution and acid rain.

3
Assessing Supports for Reasoning

This item tests your ability to recognize the difference between *adequate* and *inadequate* support, *relevant* and *irrelevant* support, or *objective* and *emotional* support for an argument. You will be given a passage to read; you will then be expected to choose a statement that offers the best support for an author's claim or choose an option that describes a support as *adequate*, *inadequate*, *relevant*, or *irrelevant*.

- Check details against the main pattern of organization. The same event will provide different relevant details based on how the ideas are organized. For example, narrative passages may include different time order details than a process that relies on ordered steps in a series.
- Check to match that generalized or broad statements are followed by specific examples or illustrations.
- Check the logic of inferences and implications by matching conclusions to evidence.

Exercises: Assessing Supports for Reasoning

PASSAGE #1
Read the passage below and answer the following questions.

1   Everywhere it occurred, industrialization drove society from an agricultural to an urban
way of life. The old system, in which peasant families worked the fields during the
summer and did their cottage industry work in the winter to their own standards and at
their own pace, slowly disappeared. In its place came urban life tied to the factory
5   system. The factory was a place where for long hours people did repetitive tasks using
machines to process large amounts of raw materials. This was an efficient way to make a
lot of high-quality goods cheaply. But the factories were often dangerous places, and the
lifestyle connected to them had a terrible effect on the human condition.

In the factory system, the workers worked, and the owners made profits. The owners
10   wanted to make the most they could from their investment and to get the most work they
could from their employees. The workers, in turn, felt that they deserved more of the
profits because their labor made production possible. This was a situation guaranteed to
produce conflict, especially given the wretched conditions the workers faced in the first
stages of industrialization.

15   The early factories were miserable places, featuring bad lighting, lack of ventilation,
dangerous machines, and frequent breakdowns. Safety standards were practically
nonexistent, and workers in various industries could expect to contract serious diseases;
for example, laborers working with lead paint developed lung problems, pewter workers
fell ill to palsy, miners suffered black lung disease, and operators of primitive machines
20   lost fingers, hands, and even lives. Not until late in the nineteenth century did health and
disability insurance come into effect. In some factories workers who suffered accidents
were deemed to be at fault; and since there was little job security, a worker could be fired
for almost any reason.

The demand for plentiful and cheap labor led to the widespread employment of women
25   and children who worked long hours. Girls as young as 6 years old were used to haul
carts of coal in Lancashire mines, and boys and girls of 5 years of age worked in textile
mills, where their nimble little fingers could easily untangle jams in the machines. When
they were not laboring, the working families lived in horrid conditions in Manchester,
England. There were no sanitary, water, or medical services for the workers,
30   and working families were crammed 12 and 15 individuals to a room in damp, dark
cellars. Bad diet, alcoholism, cholera, and typhus reduced lifespans in the industrial
cities. (Brummet, Palmira, et al. *Civilization: Past and Present*. New York: Longman,
2000)

1. Throughout the passage, which type of support is offered for the author's conclusion that "But the factories were often dangerous places, and the lifestyle connected to them had a terrible effect on the human condition" (lines 5-6)?
   A. Objective.
   B. Emotional.

2. The author's claim that "This was a situation guaranteed to produce conflict, especially given the wretched conditions the workers faced in the first stages of industrialization" (lines 12-14) is
   A. inadequately supported because it lacks evidence and explanation.
   B. adequately supported by factual details.

3. Which statement offers the best support for the author's claim that "The demand for plentiful and cheap labor led to the widespread employment of women and children who worked long hours" (lines 24-25)?
   A. Women made up the majority of the workplace in textile mills.
   B. Children were fast workers.
   C. Women worked in textile mills from 5 a.m. to 7:30 p.m.14 1/2 hours, 6 days a week.
   D. Women earned higher wages in factories than they could in other jobs.

PASSAGE #2
Read the passage below and answer the questions that follow.

1   If you have ever stayed up late, say, studying or partying, and then awakened early the next morning, you have probably experienced sleep deprivation. In fact, you may be sleep-deprived right now. If so, you have company. Many adults do not get enough sleep (defined as 8 hours). Sleep deprivation affects us in at least three important psychological
5   areas: attention, mood, and performance.

     Sleep deprivation affects the ability to perform tasks requiring sustained attention. Young adults who volunteered for a sleep deprivation study were allowed to sleep for only 5 hours each night, for a total of 7 nights. After 3 nights of restricted sleep, volunteers complained of cognitive, emotional, and physical difficulties. Moreover, their
10   performance on a visual motor task declined after only 2 nights of restricted sleep. Visual motor tasks usually require participants to concentrate on detecting a change in a particular stimulus, and then to respond as quickly as they can after they perceive the change by pressing a button. Although you may be able to perform short mental tasks normally when sleep deprived, if a task requires sustained attention and a motor response,
15   your performance will suffer. Driving a car is an example of such a task. In fact, in a survey by the National Sleep Foundation, 25% of the respondents reported that they had at some time fallen asleep at the wheel; sleepy drivers account for at least 100,000 car crashes each year.

     Moods are also affected by sleep deprivation. Those who sleep less than 6 hours each
20   weekday night are more likely to report being impatient or aggravated when faced with common minor frustrations such as being stuck in traffic or having to wait in line, and they were more dissatisfied with life in general, according to the National Sleep

86

Foundation. The loss of even one night's sleep can lead to increases in the next day's level of cortisol. Cortisol helps the body meet the demands of stress. However, sleep
25   deprivation can lead to a change in cortisol levels that, in turn, alters other biological functions. Regularly increased cortisol levels affect memory and cause a decrease in the immune system.

And what about a series of all-nighters, when you get no sleep at all, as might occur during finals period? Results from volunteers who have gone without sleep for long
30   stretches (finally sleeping after staying awake anywhere from 4 to 11 days) show profound psychological changes, such as hallucinations, feelings of losing control or going crazy, anxiety, and paranoia. Morevoer, going without sleep alters the normal circadian rhythms of changes in temperature, metabolism, and hormone secretion. Results of a study on sleep deprived humans found a different pattern of brain activation
35   when learning verbal material, compared to the pattern of activation when not sleep-deprived, suggesting an attempt to compensate for the brain changes induced by sleep deprivation. (Adapted from Kosslyn, Stephen M., and Robin S. Rosenberg. *Psychology*. Boston: Allyn and Bacon, 2004).

4. The author's claim that "Sleep deprivation affects the ability to perform tasks requiring sustained attention" (line 6) is
    A. inadequately supported based on personal opinion.
    B. adequately supported based on factual details.

5. Throughout the passage, which type of support is offered for the author's conclusion that "Sleep deprivation affects us in at least three important psychological areas: attention, mood, and performance" (lines 4-5)?
    A. Objective.
    B. Emotional.

6. Which statement offers the best support for the authors' claim that "Many adults do not get enough sleep (defined as 8 hours)" (lines 3-4)?
    A. In today's world of overscheduled lives and 10-hour workdays, no one can claim to be getting a natural amount of sleep.
    B. Older adults sleep less than younger adults and children.
    C. Many adults claim to be so sleepy during the day that their daily activities are affected.
    D. A 2002 survey by the National Sleep Foundation found that two out of three people are sleeping fewer than 6 hours each night.

PASSAGE #3
Read the passage below and answer the questions that follow.

1   Almost everyone agrees that the use of drugs to enhance sports performance is unfair. Safeguards have been put in place, and the detection of drugs in a winner's body disqualifies that person from competition.

Now comes genetic engineering. With the human genome mapped and technology
5   following rapidly, it is likely that inserting genetic materials in athletes can increase their
bulked-up muscle mass or their oxygen-carrying capacity. They will be able to run faster,
to jump higher, and to throw further. Where the record for the 26.2 mile marathon is
about 2 hours, someone may be able to run it in an hour and a half. The record for the
100-meter sprint, currently at 9.79 seconds, could drop to 6 seconds.

10   The risks to health would be high. As the president of a biomedical ethics research
institute said, inserting genetic materials "is like firing at the bull's-eye of a target with
shotgun pellets." When you inject the material, you don't know its exact effects. You
might want to strengthen the shoulder muscles of a javelin thrower, for example, but you
might enlarge that person's heart, too. Suppose that you add the gene for human growth
15   hormone, but it turns out that you can't regulate it. The individual could end up with a
gigantic head, jaw, hands, and feet.

With health risks high, would athletes take the risk? There is no doubt about the answer.
Nearly 200 U.S. athletes who were aspiring for the Olympics were asked if they would
take a banned substance that would guarantee them victory in every competition for the
20   next five years—but at the end of the five years it would cause their death. More than half
said they would take it.

As genetic manipulation becomes more like a rifle shot than a shotgun blast—and we are
closing in on that day—some athletes will seize the opportunity to increase their
advantage. Others, seeing this, will do the same. The rush for genetic manipulation will
25   be on. (Henslin, James M. *Sociology*. 6th ed. Boston: Allyn and Bacon, 2003)

7.   Throughout the passage, which type of support is offered for the author's conclusion that
"As genetic manipulation becomes more like a rifle shot than a shotgun blast—and we
are closing in on that day—some athletes will seize the opportunity to increase their
advantage" (lines 22-24)?
A. Objective
B. Emotional

8.   The author's claim that "When you inject the material, you don't know its exact effects."
(line 12) is
A. inadequately supported because it lacks evidence.
B. adequately supported with relevant details.

9.   The author's claim that "With the human genome mapped and technology
following rapidly, it is likely that inserting genetic materials in athletes can increase their
bulked-up muscle mass or their oxygen-carrying capacity" (lines 4-6) is
A. adequately supported by factual detail.
B. inadequately supported because it is based on generalizations.

10. Which statement offers the best support for the author's claim that "The risks to health would be high" (line 10)?
   A. Untested gene therapies could cause permanent damage.
   B. Genetic modifications to make muscles strong may put a strain on bones.
   C. Injecting red blood cells improves endurance, but the risks are blood clots, bacterial infection, and congestive heart failure.
   D. Injecting artificial genes to help a sprinter's muscles bulge with energy could result in pulled muscles and broken bones.

Part Three: Reading Exit Test

Read the passage below and answer the questions that follow.

Snakes, like all reptiles, are cold-blooded. They need to maintain a certain body temperature to survive. Although snakes depend on the outside environment to give them the energy they need to maintain their body temperature within the range necessary for life processes, they are not passive prisoners of the constant variations temperature.

5 Snakes can control heat exchange between their bodies and their environments by a combination of behavioral and physiological processes. For instance, a snake can control its absorption of the heat from the sun—and thereby its body temperature—by altering the color of its skin or changing the exposure of its body to the sun.

Many snakes can change their color. Because dark skin substantially increases the
10 amount of solar energy that is absorbed, many snakes living in cooler parts of an area are darker than those that live in warmer climates. Additionally, many snakes that live in warmer regions can change their color according to the amount of sun they get during changes in seasons. Some snakes use their color changing ability to increase sun exposure by having dark skin on their heads which they expose to the sun before other parts of
15 their body. Warming the brain and the sensory organs such as the eyes and the tongue first enhances a snake's ability to detect both danger and food. Finally, pregnant females of some species are darker than males and non-pregnant females to maintain warmer-than-normal body temperatures that speed up the development of embryos.

A second way that snakes control their absorption of the sun is by increasing or
20 decreasing the amount of body area exposed to the sun. The snake can make its temperature warmer than the outside air by lying at right angles to the direction of the sun and spreading and flattening to increase its body's surface area. When a snake's body has reached a suitable temperature, it avoids further heating by lightening its skin color, changing its position, and eventually moving underground. In addition, the temperature
25 of the surface that the snake is in contact with is also important because a cool snake can crawl on a warm rock or other surface and absorb its heat. (Adapted from Smith, Robert Leo, and Thomas M. Smith. *Elements of Ecology*. 5th ed. San Francisco: Benjamin Cummings, 2003)

1. Which sentence best states the main idea of this passage?
    A. Snakes live in warm and cool climates.
    B. A snake's sensory organs must be kept warm so it can eat and detect danger.
    C. Snakes are prisoners of changes in temperature.
    D. Snakes use several methods to control their absorption of heat from the sun.

2. Snakes use their color changing ability to
    A. regulate their body temperature.
    B. detect danger.
    C. attract a mate.
    D. shed their skin.

3. The primary purpose of this passage is to
    A. contrast the different ways snakes expose their bodies to the sun.
    B. inform the reader about how snakes control their body temperatures.
    C. analyze the snake's ability to adapt.
    D. describe the life cycle of snakes.

4. For this passage, the author uses an overall organizational pattern of
    A. cause and effect.
    B. process.
    C. classification.
    D. simple listing.

5. "Warming the brain and the sensory organs such as the eyes and the tongue first enhances a snake's ability to detect both danger and food." (lines 15-16)

    The relationship of parts within the sentence above is
    A. example.
    B. time order.
    C. cause and effect.
    D. addition.

6. As used in line 4, passive most nearly means
    A. agreeable
    B. nonviolent
    C. tame
    D. submissive

7. The tone of this passage can best be described as
    A. admiring.
    B. objective.
    C. convincing.
    D. respectful.

8. The author's claim that "the snake can make its temperature warmer than the outside air by lying at right angles to the direction of the sun and spreading and flattening to increase its body's surface area" is
    A. inadequately supported because it lacks evidence and explanation.
    B. adequately supported by factual evidence.

9. "Finally, pregnant females of some species are darker than males and nonpregnant females to maintain warmer-than-normal body temperatures that speed up the development of embryos."

The above sentence is a statement of
A. fact.
B. opinion.

Read the passage below and answer the questions that follow.

Spielberg's journey is one version of the universal story of human development: A skinny kid beset by fears and with few friends becomes one of the most powerful figures in the global entertainment industry; from a family with a fragmented family life develops a man's resolve to make the best possible life for his own family.

5   Steven Spielberg was a perpetual new kid on the block. His father, Arnold, a pioneer in the use of computers in engineering, was hardly every around and, to make matters worse, frequently uprooted his family, moving from Ohio to New Jersey, to Arizona, and finally to Northern California. He was also, by all accounts, an unusual child, both in his appearance (he had a large head and protruding ears) and in his fearful and awkward
10 behavior. Spielberg himself has said that he "felt like an alien" throughout his childhood. He desperately wanted to be accepted but didn't fit in. So, at age 12 he began making films. Spielberg continued to make movies as a teenager, which helped him gain acceptance by his peers.

When he was 16, Spielberg's parents divorced, and Spielberg blamed his father's
15 constant traveling for the breakup. His father remarried which deepened Spielberg's unhappiness; he couldn't stand his father's second wife. Although he withdrew from his father, he remained close with his mother, Leah, a concert pianist and artist. His split with his father lasted some 15 years.

In many ways, Spielberg's films, like the rest of his life, are shaped by his childhood.
20 Spielberg himself has said about *E.T., The Extra-Terrestrial*, "The whole movie is really about divorce . . . . Henry's (the main character's) ambition to find a father by bringing E.T. into his life to fill some black hole—that was my struggle to find somebody to replace the dad who I felt had abandoned me." Many of Spielberg's other films include children who are separated from their parents (such as the girl in *Poltergeist* and the boy
25 in *Close Encounters of the Third Kind*). *Back to the Future* might represent his longings to change the past, if only he could. As he matured, Spielberg's identification with oppressed people in general, not just oppressed children, led him to make movies such as *The Color Purple, Schlindler's List*, and *Amistad*.

Steven Spielberg married and had a child, but eventually divorced his first wife, actress
30 Amy Irving. His own experiences made him extremely sensitive to the effect of the divorce on his son, Max, and he made every attempt to ensure that Max did not feel abandoned. When he married again, he became deeply involved with his family, which

includes seven children, some of them adopted. His father Arnold became a well-loved grandfather as well. (Adapted from Kosslyn, Stephen M. and Robin S. Rosenberg. *Psychology*. 2nd ed. Boston: Allyn and Bacon, 2004)

10. Which sentence best states the main idea of this passage?
    A. Spielberg identifies with oppressed peoples.
    B. Spielberg's films are based on his childhood.
    C. Spielberg's difficult childhood shaped his career as a filmmaker and his personal life as a husband and a father.
    D. Spielberg's life was deeply affected by his father's abandonment of the family.

11. The author's primary purpose is to
    A. explain how Spielberg was affected by his childhood.
    B. tell the story of Spielberg's childhood.
    C. persuade the reader of Spielberg's greatness.
    D. illustrate Spielberg's achievements.

12. "He was also, by all accounts, an unusual child, both in his appearance (he had a large head and protruding ears) and in his fearful and awkward behavior." (lines 8-10)

    The relationship of the parts within the sentence above is
    A. comparison.
    B. example.
    C. cause and effect.
    D. addition.

13. "He desperately wanted to be accepted but didn't fit in. So, at age 12 he began making films." (lines 11-12)

    Identify the relationship between these two sentences from paragraph two.
    A. comparison/contrast
    B. cause and effect
    C. statement/clarification
    D. time order

14. In this passage, the author shows bias in favor of
    A. divorce and remarriage.
    B. adoption.
    C. making movies about oppressed peoples.
    D. using childhood lessons to improve one's adult life.

15. What is the overall tone of this passage?
    A. optimistic
    B. nostalgic
    C. sad
    D. authoritative

16. *"Back to the Future* might represent his longings to change the past, if only he could."

The above sentence is a statement of
A.   fact.
B.   opinion.

17.   A conclusion that can be drawn from the fourth paragraph is that Spielberg's movies
A.   were very successful.
B.   used children as focal points.
C.   were about the hardships of oppressed people.
D.   were shaped by his childhood.

18.   In the second paragraph, which type of support is offered for the author's claim that "Steven Spielberg was a perpetual new kid on the block." (line 5)
A. objective
B. emotional

Read the passage below and answer the questions that follow.

There had been great athletes before; indeed probably the greatest all-around athlete of the twentieth century was Jim Thorpe, a Sac and Fox Indian who won both the pentathalon and the decathalon at the 1912 Olympic Games, made Walter Camp's All-American football team in 1912 and 1913, then played major league baseball for several
5   years before becoming a pioneer founder and player in the National Football League. But what truly made the 1920s a golden age was a coincidence—the emergence in a few short years of a remarkable collection of what today would be called superstars.

In football there was the University of Illinois's Harold "Red" Grange, who averaged over 10 yards a carry during his college career and who in one incredible quarter during
10   the 1924 game between Illinois and Michigan carried the ball four times and scored a touchdown each time, gaining in the process 263 yards. In prize fighting, heavyweight champion Jack Dempsey, the "Manassas Mauler," knocked out a succession of challengers in bloody battles only to be deposed in 1927 by "Gentleman Gene" Tunney, who gave him a 15-round boxing lesson and then, according to Tunney's own account,
15   celebrated by consuming "several pots of tea."

During the same years, William "Big Bill" Tilden dominated tennis, winning the national singles title every year from 1920 to 1925 along with nearly every other tournament he entered. Beginning in 1923, Robert T. "Bobby" Jones ruled over the world of golf with equal authority, his climactic achievement being his capture of the amateur and open
20   championships of both the United States and Great Britain in 1930.

A few women athletes dominated their sports during the Golden Age in similar fashion. In tennis Helen Wills was three times United States singles champion and the winner of the women's singles at Wimbledon eight times in the late 1920s and early 1930s. The swimmer Gertrude Ederle, holder of 18 world records by the time she was 17, swam the

25   English Channel on her second attempt, in 1926. She was not only the first woman to do so, but she did it faster than any of the four men who had previously made it across.

However, the sports star among stars was "the Sultan of Swat," baseball's Babe Ruth. Ruth not only dominated baseball, he changed it from a game ruled by pitchers and low scores to one in which hitting was more greatly admired. Originally himself a brilliant

30   pitcher, his incredible hitting ability made him more valuable in the outfield, where he could play every day. Before Ruth, John "Home Run" Baker was the most famous slugger; his greatest home run total was 12, achieved shortly before the Great War. Ruth hit 29 in 1919 and 54 in 1920, his first year with the New York Yankees. By 1923, he was so feared that he was given a base on balls more than half the times he appeared at

35   the plate. (Garrary, John A., and Mark C. Carnes. *The American Nation*. New York: Longman, 2000)

19.   Which sentence best states the main idea of the passage?
     A.   Sports became popular after World War I.
     B.   The 1920s was the Golden Age for athletic superstars.
     C.   Basketball, tennis, and football became popular sports in the 1920s.
     D.   Babe Ruth symbolizes the ideal athlete of the 1920s.

20.   According to the passage, Gertrude Ederle
     A.   was a champion tennis player.
     B.   competed with men in swimming.
     C.   successfully swam the English Channel.
     D.   held 17 records by the time she was 18.

21.   For the passage, the author uses the overall organizational pattern that
     A.   gives examples of the achievements of star athletes of the 1920s.
     B.   compares men's and women's sports accomplishments.
     C.   states the reasons sports were so popular in the 1920s.
     D.   lists the record holders in 1920s athletics.

22.   The author's primary purpose is to
     A.   entertain the reader with stories about 1920s athletes.
     B.   describe the lives of athletes in the 1920s.
     C.   argue that the Golden Age was the best sports decade in history.
     D.   inform the reader of the accomplishments of athletes in the Golden Age.

23.   "There had been great athletes before; indeed probably the greatest all-around athlete of the twentieth century was Jim Thorpe, a Sac and Fox Indian who won both the pentathalon and the decathalon at the 1912 Olympic Games, made Walter Camp's All-American football team in 1912 and 1913, then played major league baseball for several years before becoming a pioneer founder and player in the National Football League."

What is the relationship between the parts of the following sentence?
A.　summary
B.　example
C.　listing
D.　contrast

24.　As used in line 19, <u>climactic</u> most nearly means
A.　exciting.
B.　final.
C.　impressive.
D.　extreme

25.　The author shows bias in favor of
A.　1920s athletic superstars.
B.　women athletes of the Golden Age.
C.　prizefight heavyweight champions.
D.　Babe Ruth, the "Sultan of Sweat."

26.　"Ruth hit 29 in 1919 and 54 in 1920, his first year with the New York Yankees." (lines 32-33)

The above sentence is a statement of
A.　fact.
B.　opinion.

27.　The author's claim that "a few women athletes dominated their sports during the Golden Age in similar fashion" (line 21) is
A.　adequately supported with relevant details.
B.　inadequately supported based on personal opinion.

Read the passage below and answer the questions that follow.

Public opinion polling sounds scientific with its talk of random samples and sampling error; it is easy to take results for solid fact. But being an informed consumer of polls requires more than just a nuts and bolts knowledge of how they are conducted; you should think about whether the questions are fair and unbiased before making too much
5　of the results. The good—or the harm—that polls do depends on how well the data are collected and how thoughtfully the data are interpreted.

Political scientist Benjamin Ginsberg has even argued that polls weaken democracy. He says that polls permit the government to think that it has taken public opinion into account when only passive, often ill-informed opinions have been counted. Polls
10　substitute passive attitudes for active expressions of opinion, such as voting and letter writing, which take work. Responding to a poll taker is a lazy way to claim that "my voice has been heard."

Polls can also weaken democracy by distorting the election process. They are often accused of creating a *bandwagon effect*. This term refers to voters who support a

96

15 candidate merely because they see that others are doing so. Although only 2 percent of
people in a recent CBS/*New York Times* poll said that poll results had influenced them,
26 percent said they thought others had been influenced (showing that Americans feel
"It's always the other person who's susceptible.") Beyond this, polls play to the media's
interest in who's hot and who's not. The issues of recent presidential campaigns have
20 sometimes been drowned out by a steady flood of poll results.

Perhaps the most extensive criticism of polling is that by altering the wording of a
question, pollsters can get pretty much the results they want. Sometimes subtle changes
in question wording can produce dramatic differences. For example, a month before the
start of the Gulf War, the percentage of the public who thought we should go to war was
25 18 percentage points higher in the ABC/*Washington Post* poll than the CBS/*New York
Times* poll. The former poll asked whether the United States should go to war "at some
point after January 15 or not," a relatively vague question; in contrast, the latter poll
offered an alternative to war, asking whether the "U.S. should start military actions
against Iraq, or should the U.S. wait longer to see if the trade embargo and other
30 economic sanctions work." It is, therefore, important to evaluate carefully how questions
are posed when reading public opinion data. (Adapted from Edwards, George C., Martin
P. Wattenberg, and Robert L. Lineberry. *Government in America*. 9th ed. New York:
Longman, 2000)

28. Which sentence best states the main idea of the passage?
   A.   Polls are scientific.
   B.   Polls are not always accurate representations of fact.
   C.   Polls have no validity.
   D.   The print media uses polls to influence readers.

29. The implied main idea of paragraph three is
   A.   people admit that they are influenced by polls.
   B.   presidential candidates make decisions based on polls.
   C.   poll results are used as news items by the media.
   D.   polls influence people to vote for candidates that others like.

30. According to the passage, some people who respond to polls
   A.   are ill-informed.
   B.   are well-educated.
   C.   understand the bias of polls.
   D.   use polls as a substitute for voting.

31. For this passage, the author uses an overall organizational pattern that
   A.   gives results of polls.
   B.   describes how polls are conducted.
   C.   suggests reasons polls may be harmful.
   D.   defines public opinion polls.

32. What is the relationship between the parts of the following sentence?

"The former poll asked whether the United States should go to war "at some point after January 15 or not," a relatively vague question; in contrast, the latter poll offered an alternative to war, asking whether the "U. S. should start military actions against Iraq, or should the U. S. wait longer to see if the trade embargo and other economic sanctions work." (lines 26-30)
   A.   cause and effect
   B.   time order
   C.   contrast
   D.   addition

33. Identify the relationship between these two sentences in paragraph three.

"They are often accused of creating a *bandwagon effect*. This term refers to voters who support a candidate merely because they see that others are doing so." (lines 13-15)
   A.   example
   B.   comparison
   C.   summary
   D.   definition

34. The word <u>subtle</u> (line 22) means
   A.   careless
   B.   slight
   C.   foolish
   D.   simple

35. In this passage, the author is biased for
   A.   manipulating poll data.
   B.   using polls to determine popularity of candidates.
   C.   being an informed consumer of polls.
   D.   media reporting of poll results.

36. The author's claim that "political scientist Benjamin Ginsberg has even argued that polls weaken democracy" (line 7) is
   A.   inadequate support because it depends on personal opinion.
   B.   adequate support based on factual evidence.

Part Four: Student Answer Sheets

WORKBOOK TEST ANSWER SHEET

Student Name: _____   Date: _____

Workbook: _____

Chapter and Skill: _____

1. _____   2 _____   3. _____   4. _____   5. _____   6. _____

7. _____   8. _____   9. _____   10. _____   11. _____   12. _____

13. _____   14. _____   15. _____   16. _____   17. _____   18. _____

19. _____   20. _____

Thinking Through the Test: My thoughts about my answers and my performance:

_____

_____

_____

_____

_____

_____

_____

_____

_____

READING TEST ANSWER SHEET

Student Name: _____   Date: _____

Test: _____

1. _____   2. _____   3. _____   4. _____   5. _____   6. _____

7. _____   8. _____   9. _____   10. _____   11. _____   12. _____

13. _____   14. _____   15. _____   16. _____   17. _____   18. _____

19. _____   20. _____   21. _____   22. _____   23. _____   24. _____

25. _____   26, _____   27. _____   28. _____   29. _____   30. _____

31. _____   32. _____   33. _____   34. _____   35. _____   36. _____

Thinking Through the Test: My thoughts about my answers and my performance.

_____

_____

_____

_____

_____

_____

_____

_____

NOTES

NOTES

NOTES

NOTES

NOTES

NOTES